MW00962678

Celebrate!

The Washington Post guide to successful celebrations

Virginia Rodriguez

For Anita and Bob

◆

Published by
The Washington Post
1150 15th Street, NW
Washington, DC 20071

◆

© 2004 by The Washington Post

No part of this book may be reproduced or transmitted in any form
or by any means, electronic or mechanical, including photocopying,
recording, or by any information storage and retrieval system,
without written permission from the publisher.

The body copy is set in Janson and Frutiger.
The display type is Sloop Script Medium.

Manufactured by Chroma Graphics, Largo, Md.,
in association with Alan Abrams.

ISBN: 1-930691-04-1

PUBLISHERS:
Lionel Neptune and Cecelia Stephens

EDITOR:
Noel Epstein

BOOK DESIGN & PRODUCTION:
Lianne U. Liang

RESEARCH:
Susan Breitkopf and Julie Katz

ASSISTANTS:
Karen Hill and Judy Sieber

PHOTOGRAPHS:
Tulip photo - © Orion Press/CORBIS

Acknowledgments

◆

ALTHOUGH I AM, of course, solely responsible for the contents of this book, I am deeply indebted to many for their help. Susan Brietkopf and Julie Katz, for example, did stellar jobs of research and, if that weren't enough, offered sound feedback and personal support. Similarly, Karen Hill and Judy Sieber provided valuable help, especially for the Directory of Service Providers. I am also grateful to Cecelia Stephens and Lionel Neptune for overseeing this project.

Marianne Becton, Rima Calderon, Nancy Chistolini, Alice Conway, Linda Erdos, Colleen Evans, Linda Levey Grossman and Jennifer Cover Payne are consummate professionals in their respective fields, and I am honored that they were willing to contribute their advice and opinions to *Celebrate!* I am fortunate to have worked with all of them, but, more importantly, I am blessed to call them friends.

Many members of the International Special Events Society and the National Association of Catering Executives were kind enough to participate in our survey and to offer advice, and I am grateful for their assistance. Sara Hayter Franklin of Northern Virginia Bridal Services (and formerly of Design Cuisine) and Beverly Brockus, a public relations professional and longtime colleague, also generously shared their knowledge and expertise, which were greatly appreciated.

This book would not have been possible without those who took the time from their hectic schedules to talk with me, share their ideas and part with valuable suggestions. You will find them throughout the pages of *Celebrate!*

My heartfelt thanks go to Lianne Liang of Liang Publication and Production Services and Robert Rodriguez, senior writer in *The Washington Post*'s Creative Services Department before he retired in 1997. (Yes, we are related…married for almost 30 years.) Their considerable talents have combined to create striking cover and text designs, resulting in a distinctively appealing publication. I am indebted to them for this.

Very special thanks go to the late John Dower, who hired me at the *Post*, to Marcelino Fernandez and Bill Homan, whom I consider my generous mentors, to Lillie Lee, my friend and colleague for almost 30 years, and to Liz Hylton and Chip Knight, who have long provided me with good counsel on many matters. And I am especially grateful to the late Katharine Graham, who allowed me to learn from her style and grace.

There simply are no words to express my gratitude to Noel Epstein, my editor and my friend. He is a remarkable human being, and his love of the English language and enthusiasm for his work are evident throughout the book. He has guided every thought, every word, every page. He is an exceptional editor. Although he wonders if I will ever remember to put like things together as I write, I have taken away much from working with him, not the least of which is what he learned from watching his wife Anita and their daughters plan two weddings.   ◆

Contents

◆

The Times of Your Life

Gather moments while you may
Collect the dreams you dream today
Remember, will you remember
The times of your life?

— BILL LANE AND ROGER NICHOLS
Times of Your Life

THIS BOOK is about rejoicing, about not only remembering but celebrating the times of our lives from birth through every age, about sharing it all with family and friends and having one heck of a time in the process. *Celebrate!* is opposed to those who spend lots of time grumbling. The trick in life is to do the best we can with the hand we are dealt—and to celebrate our blessings and milestones and friendships along the way.

The book's more practical aim is to help you with all the rejoicing, particularly with what you need to know and find in the Washington area to celebrate births and birthdays, bar and bat mitzvahs, Quinceaneras and Sweet 16s, debutante balls and graduation parties, weddings and anniversaries, reunions and retirements, New Year's Eve and July 4th and other milestones, holidays and friendships.

The biggest bash in most of our lives, of course, is a wedding, which is why endless books have been written about wedding planning. Unfortunately, though, none is tailored for those of us in the national capital area. *Celebrate!* aims to correct that. Most of its chapters contain information that is useful for Washington-area weddings, and a separate weddings chapter is about subjects that are unique to that big day, such as the many routes by which Washingtonians can search for the perfect wedding dress. In addition, the book's special sur-vey of what 60 local event professionals deem the area's best venues and vendors, plus its Directory of Service Providers, serve up lots more Washington-area information to fill the void.

ALL THOSE OTHER FESTIVITIES

What also has been missing, however, is a local guide for all the other celebrating and entertaining that we do. As important as weddings are, after all, they certainly are not the only occasions in our lives that call for serious celebrating. Bar and bat mitzvahs and Quinceaneras, for instance, are some-times almost as elaborate as weddings, and some milestone birthdays, anniversaries, renewals of vows and other festivities are not far behind.

Rita Bloom of Creative Parties in Bethesda, Maryland, for example, told of a 75th birthday party she did for a client's wife that focused on the wife's life as an artist. The party was held at the National Museum of Women in the Arts. The invitation was in the form of an artist's palette. The artist's work was displayed on easels everywhere during the party, and art was involved in other ways. It was no small undertaking. Or consider one couple who celebrated their 25th wedding anniversary by renewing their vows—with a black-tie affair that was as elegant as an original wedding. Indeed, a friend of mine who was there was so moved by the event that he asked his wife if she would like to do the same thing, despite the heavy expense. (His wife, however, quickly dashed that prospect, saying: "To tell you the truth, I'd rather redo the bathroom.")

Some people throw other sizable bashes for themselves. For her 50th birthday, for example, *Washington Post* real estate editor Nancy McKeon did just that, though guests did make special contributions. One showed up with a Polaroid camera and film, a couple of photo albums, colored markers and glitter. "He instructed guests to take pictures, write captions or create whatever they fancied. It was a great icebreaker, and everyone had a terrific time contributing their special picture or note to the albums, which I love," McKeon said.

Another friend threw herself a graduation party—to celebrate a master's degree that she received after a 25-year hiatus from a college campus. She held the blast for family and friends at a local restaurant cum billiard parlor cum video game emporium. Boisterous? Yes. Fun? You bet. Everyone gathered for cocktails and hors d'oeuvres. A buffet dinner followed. As guests finished their meal, the tables on which they were served turned into pool and shuffleboard tables, and the men dove into both games with gusto. Teenagers in the group headed for the arcade, which had every conceivable electronic game and virtual experience. Other guests remained in the private area where dinner had been served to loll over coffee and dessert. One and all had a delightful time.

There will always be some souls, of course, who insist that no parties be given for them—and who mean it. Their loved ones, though, still can find ways to celebrate their lives. Take the case of another couple I know who fall in this category. Instead of a party for her husband's 50th birthday, his wife surprised him at a family dinner with a beautifully wrapped box. He found it filled with a trove of tributes, humorous recollections and momentos—keepsakes, photo collages, scrapbooks—that she had solicited over an extended period from many friends, and his sons had compiled a CD of family photos and set it to music, with captions for each frame. The husband then surprised his wife on her 50th birthday—with a memory quilt, made by a quilting friend of his wife and consisting of about 30 blocks filled with contributions from family and friends. Six blocks were devoted to photos—baby snapshots, wedding pictures, family shots, college graduation photos and the like. Several blocks contained messages, while others had such memorabilia as her college tassel and a patch from her high school uniform, surrounded by classmates' signatures. Both husband and wife clearly went to considerable and heartwarming lengths to celebrate their lives and their love.

Mostly the way we celebrate, however, is with parties, and even the most elementary of these has become more imaginative. When I was growing up in New York, for example, a birthday party was a simple affair in your apartment with cake and party hats. Today there are parties where children ride ponies, dig for dinosaur fossils or pet animals. There are parties with puppet shows, clowns, magicians, face painters or balloon sculptors. There are create-your-own parties at places like the four Build-a-Bear workshops in Maryland and Virginia (where children design and take home their own Teddy bears, complete with birth certificates), Creative Cakes in Silver Spring, Maryland, (where, along with much else, they decorate the confections as well as eat them), and the seven area workshops of The Clay Cafe and Made by You (where you paint your own pottery). In addition to spending a pretty penny, parents can put in lots of effort on these—contracting with people, ensuring enough adult supervision, checking on children's food restrictions, getting other parents to sign permission slips if the party is at a recreation site like a riding stable, skating rink or moon bounce.

Similarly, many Sweet 16 parties are not the simple get-togethers I recall from youth. One parent I know, for example, used the spoils of a fundraising auction that entitled him to dinner for a group at a hip new Washington restaurant. His daughter was ecstatic to invite friends to celebrate her 16th birthday at the latest chi-chi place. Another friend rented a suite at the local Holiday Inn and invited her daughter's friends for a sleepover. Twenty-five girls had a dreamy time talking about boys, eating pizza and confiding their deepest secrets until the wee hours. Finally, the catering director of one Washington hotel recalled a Sweet 16 she recently coordinated. The teenager arrived at the hotel alone to arrange for a lunch in her honor and 40 guests. She handled all the details for the luncheon and menu, arranged for spa visits that included manicures and makeup tips for all, and insisted that the smoothies bar she also chose be staffed by a "very cute" guy. (Well, some things never change.)

Celebrations honoring prospective brides and grooms have also been evolving. Once upon a time, for example, a bachelor party was often a raucous affair, the thought of which could make brides-to-be shudder, while bachelorette parties were all-female get-togethers. Today, male and female friends often join forces with the couple, and all celebrate together. Men who still prefer to do things separately often organize "grooms' dinners" for a dozen or so people. Drinks and a game of billiards, darts or a wine tasting, followed by a gourmet dinner and wine, are among the newest trends. Coffee and liqueurs and some poker often follow. The Hotel George has a room complete with a billiards table for the before-dinner gathering and drinks, and The Chimney Room in the Ritz Carlton Georgetown is a unique space for such affairs.

SAVING MONEY AND OTHER IDEAS

Some of these and other festivities obviously can get quite expensive, but there are also less costly ways to celebrate. Teas, for example, have become popular again and are an economical as well as enchanting way to entertain. Many historic mansions and hotels in the area offer teas, and one firm, African American Tea Praises, serves themed teas

highlighting African American heritage. There are other ways to save money as well, as you will learn from this book. A chapter that examines the often-entrancing venues available for your celebrations notes one hotel, for example, where you can get lots for less. Another chapter looks at how catering costs can be lowered, and still another examines economical alternatives to fresh flowers.

Finding ways to save is just one of the values of *Celebrate!*, which provides a wide array of useful ideas and information. The book opens with possible venues for your celebrations, beginning with area hotels and historic mansions and inns. It then turns to advice about entertaining at home, followed by counsel for those who want to party in exotic and often faraway spots. The destinations noted are most commonly for weddings—including some unusual local ones like a cave or mid-air (while skydiving).

Many Washingtonians, however, are not natives and sometimes go home to celebrate. One fellow ex-New Yorker, for example, had an extraordinary time when his wife threw a surprise 60th birthday party for him at a Manhattan dance club and when his daughters rented a bus and driver for a "roots" tour of his old Brooklyn stomping grounds the next day. The dance club affair, which included dinner and a floor show, was attended not only by relatives and friends who had traveled considerable distances but also by "kids" from his old New York neighborhood. The Brooklyn tour included lunch from the famous Stage Delicatessen, served on the bus, and a stop at the site of his wedding, which was as much of a kick for his daughters as for his wife and himself.

The overwhelming majority of us, though, of course hold our parties locally, and many of the area service providers that may be needed—party planners and caterers, florists and musicians, photographers and equipment renters, bakers and stationers and transportation companies—are examined in ensuing chapters. Then, in addition to our survey of professionals' preferences, I have added a special feature. I asked eight colleagues—friends with entertaining experience ranging from modest dinner parties to gatherings of hundreds for fundraisers or corporate affairs—to provide their wisdom. They have offered some unique notions on such things (again) as ways to save money and what one calls "the Cinderella Complex"—the determination of Washingtonians to get home before midnight. In other words, the book serves up not just my advice but that of many others who have entertained professionally.

I do not mean to suggest that the book covers every conceivable kind of celebration or venue. It does not. It does not, for example, delve into the many other sites where parties can be held. For the fitness-minded, for instance, celebrating a birthday at a local health club, complete with tips for all from a personal trainer, is an ideal way to salute someone who is heading over the hill. A visit to a spa for a massage, manicure, pedicure and the like is also quite popular for a variety of celebrations, including bridal showers and bachelorette parties. For children, parties also are held at places like area gyms, to say nothing of various museums, restaurants and other sites. The choices are almost endless.

Nor does the book delve into celebrations for some events, whether a rite of passage like a memorial service, an ethnic holiday like the Chinese, Korean and Vietnamese Lunar New Year, or other occasions. This is, in part, because so much of what is in this book can be applied to most any celebration.

WHO NEEDS SPECIAL OCCASIONS?

In any case, my view is that you really don't need special occasions to celebrate. Rather, you should sometimes gather family and friends just for the joy of it. For example:

◆ **A COUNTRY WEEKEND.** Spend a weekend in the country. Hunt Country Celebrations in Fauquier County, Virginia, packages two nights' lodging at The Grey Horse Inn or another historic inn or bed and breakfast. On Friday night enjoy a picnic supper supplied by The Farm Store in The Plains and tickets to the polo matches in Great Meadow. On Saturday, after a gourmet breakfast, spend a leisurely morning in the Inn's garden or on the balcony of the Shenandoah Room reading a novel, watching trains go by or just gazing at wild flowers. In the afternoon tour local wineries, take a drive or browse local antique shops. Saturday dinner can be enjoyed at one of many fine restaurants, or you can take a short walk from the Grey Horse to the Rail Stop, once owned by actor Robert Duvall. After a sumptuous Sunday breakfast, head home relaxed and refreshed.

◆ **POTOMAC CRUISES.** Get a group together and split the cost of a cruise on the Potomac. Many ships are available for scheduled cruises, but the Potomac Belle, docked at the City Dock in Old Town Alexandria, offers privacy for your group in intimate surroundings. The vessel is certified to carry up to 49 passengers. In cooler months, when the top deck generally can't be used, the main salon can accommodate up to 25 passengers. The boat is rented for two-hour minimums. A sound system is available for taped music, and a caterer from the ship's approved list must be retained to provide food and beverage.

◆ **A BLOCK PARTY.** Throw a block party, or neighborhood bash, to celebrate the diversity of your community. It's a great way to welcome newcomers and to catch up with longtime neighbors. Instead of typical American fare or potluck dishes, ask everyone to prepare a dish related to their ethnic background. Like festivals celebrating heritages and customs, a party highlighting the food of various cultures is a perfect way to encourage friendship in your community and to promote understanding of different cultures.

In short, surround yourself with family and friends, cherish every day, and celebrate life every chance you get.

◆

CHAPTER I

Satisfying Settings

*The only place where your dream becomes
impossible is in your own thinking.*

—ROBERT H. SCHULLER

THERE ARE MAGICAL spaces, historic places and many other attractive settings for your celebrations in the Washington area. The choices range from cozy inns to glittering hotels to mansions and community halls. They are available in every price range, and wonderful weddings, bar or bat mitzvahs, renewals of vows, reunions, fundraisers and many other affairs can be held in them.

Washington is blessed, for example, with luxury hotels. The Mayflower, the Willard, the Hay Adams—they exude elegance and history. The challengers—the Ritz Carlton, Washington, (and its sister hotels in Georgetown and in Pentagon City and Tysons Corner, Virginia), the Fairmont, the Four Seasons, the St. Regis, the Park Hyatt— aren't steeped in the historical significance of those grand dames. However, they surely offer elegant settings, the finest in food and wonderful service. Washington also has excellent mid-priced hotels, including the J.W. Marriott, the Hilton Washington & Towers and the Renaissance Washington, and you can even find a low-cost hotel, like the Holiday Inn in Leesburg, Virginia, with unusual charm and value. *(See boxes on pp. 14 and 17.)*

All, moreover, offer what hotels provide—convenience. Everything you need usually is right there, from event and social coordinators to caterers to whatever else is required to orchestrate as effortless an occasion as possible. Not having to work with an army of vendors keeps details—and stress—to a minimum, no small benefit.

For a wedding, a hotel can accommodate the ceremony and the reception. Rooms for out-of-towners are on-site, as is the honeymoon suite, and both usually are offered at reduced rates. You also can do whatever other entertaining goes along with weddings—rehearsal dinners, day-after brunches and the like—on the spot. Accomplishing all of this in one lovely, comfortable place also cuts down on transportation expenses, which can be significant, at least if you need frequent service. You might even cut the cost of your honeymoon trip as well. In exchange for your business, some hotels offer such incentives as reduced prices or upgrades at sister properties—some in exotic locales—that might otherwise be out of your price range.

In addition, good hotels have seasoned event coordinators. For example, Ritz Carlton Hotels have a special person to manage social events ranging from baby namings to 50th anniversary parties and everything in between. Bob Mikolitch of the St. Regis has particular experience helping couples plan weddings, often growing close to them as he gets involved in their arrangements and their lives. "After the wedding, I feel like I've lost two of my best friends," he says. That's the kind of experience and service you want.

As for prices, hotel weddings can range from the surprisingly low-cost to the staggeringly expensive. Every hotel chain has Washington-area facilities, and most have public spaces for almost any type of celebration. Be sure to inquire, however, about minimums. It is not unusual for some hotels to require minimum outlays of tens of thousands of dollars or more for food and beverages, especially on Saturday nights during the busiest seasons.

Though the Holiday Inn-Leesburg is the kind of bargain that you sometimes can find, you generally get what you pay for. A low-cost, seated dinner usually will have the first course preset on the table, and guests will receive a pre-plated entrée. At most

LOTS FOR LESS:

Holiday Inn-Leesburg

There's a song that keeps wafting through my head when I think of the Holiday Inn at historic Carradoc Hall, in Leesburg, Virginia: "There's a small hotel/with a wishing well/I wish that we were there, together." It's that kind of place, down to the single candles in the windows of the old mansion.

The other thing that keeps going through my head is how little everything costs there.

Carradoc Hall, an historic site connected to the Holiday Inn, has a separate entrance and four wonderful guestrooms. The Mansion House Restaurant also has four rooms complete with original flooring. The space, which is beautifully done in colonial décor, circa 1747, won't work for a seated dinner except for small parties, but it does work well for a larger stand-up reception. Fireplaces can be lighted, and the rooms can be smashing, particularly when decorated for the fall and winter holiday seasons.

The main building houses the Grand Ballroom, an outside covered terrace, The Tavern and the adjacent Garden Room.

The Grand Ballroom is dark and of the cookie-cutter variety, with run-of-the-mill carpeting and wall coverings. It accommodates 300 for a seated lunch or dinner, 250 with dancing. Creative lighting, however, could make all the difference in this room. The adjacent covered terrace makes a decent setting for a pre-dinner reception, particularly in good weather. Reject the hotel's suggestion, however, to use the space as a wedding ceremony site—unless it can guarantee that it will block the annoying traffic noise from nearby Route 7. Just down the steps from the terrace is a gazebo, situated among lovely grounds that are perfect for picture taking (though they, too, are strikingly close to Route 7). The Loudoun Room accommodates 120 guests.

The Tavern will seat up to 36. You can spill out into the Garden Room for a little more seating and dancing. It has a stone floor. But these spaces can only be utilized together on a Sunday evening, and there's no guarantee that a hotel guest won't stop by to help celebrate.

The banquet food at the Holiday Inn is good. The staff is friendly and well trained. Parking is plentiful, there's a shuttle service to Dulles Airport, and best of all, the price is right!

low-cost hotels, the food won't be gourmet, the room distinctive or the service French. But service still can be gracious and smooth, at least if you pay some attention to the question of wait staff. Ask if the staff works on an on-call basis or is permanent and, if permanent, the length of employment (as a rule, the longer the staff has worked, the better the service).

Costs will be affected, of course, by many other factors as well, and they can add up quickly. There can be a sizable per-guest cost spread between a chicken and beef entrée. The length of bar service and the quality of beverages obviously will affect your bill, as will whether you serve wine with dinner or you try to enhance a ho-hum room with trees, backdrops or other devices. (Actually, good lighting and the right touch of candlelight can transform an ordinary room into one of warmth and charm.)

Even in more expensive hotels, though, don't assume that because you enjoyed a meal in the hotel restaurant, you will have the same quality food and service at your affair. Many hotels have separate kitchens for restaurant and banquet facilities. Unless you have a very small party, the banquet staff may accommodate you. (One exception is the Hotel George, whose award-winning chef, Jeffrey Buben, attends to all hotel dining operations. Whether you choose the trendy restaurant Bistro Bis or decide to eat in your room, you will be served the same exceptional food.) Be sure to ask your representative to explain how the hotel you are considering operates in this regard. Ask, too, if it is possible to observe a banquet function and to taste from the menu being served, which can be done unobtrusively in the kitchen. If you require kosher food, be sure the hotel's banquet kitchen is certified as kosher; kosher caterers, among others, can identify your options (See p. 38).

Finally, keep in mind that hotels, particularly larger ones, routinely schedule multiple events. You do not want your celebration to be interrupted by the local barber shop quartet competition, so be sure to ask what else will be going on in the hotel on the day of your affair, and when and where in the facility. Any noise or crowd infringement should be thoroughly discussed, not the least of which is ample parking, and contingency plans should be made, including the hotel's responsibility to accommodate you at another comparable site if necessary. The same goes for renovations that could disrupt your celebration or cause inadequate parking. Most hotels are keen for your business and are willing to make concessions on such matters, but discussing these things in advance always leads to better relationships.

So You Want a Mansion

If you would like your guests to have a more fairy-tale-like experience, the Washington region has magnificent mansions aplenty in which to hold your celebration. Beautiful old houses with water views, or restored historic buildings overlooking just about any landscape you can think of, are yours for the renting at prices that range from reasonable to outrageous. Part of the rental fees for some historic and nonprofit venues, however, are tax deductible, so be sure to check on that question when you explore such sites.

If you take this route, you and/or your planner and guests won't have the conveniences of a hotel, which means that you will deal with many more details yourself, including air conditioning and central heating (it is essential to check on such infrastructure matters). That is what you trade for the many enchanting atmospheres that are available. For a wedding, for example, you can have the ceremony at the water's edge, at the foot of a mountain, in a giant meadow or in the drawing room of a Civil War mansion. Let your imagination run free, and you can find the place of your dreams.

Like most dreams, however, there also are all the realities that you must face. In addition to the fee for the site, you will have to arrange for everything else to be rented. That means food, beverages, tables, chairs, linens, china, cutlery, glassware, dance floors—everything required for your guests. If you choose an outdoor site, you may also have to rent a tent and/or a marquis, depending on weather conditions (although tents are needed at some hotels, too). This is, of course, in addition to music, flowers, cakes or any special effects that you might wish to include to make your occasion unique.

Restrictions are likely to apply as well. Most sites have preferred caterers, so you may not be able to use the one of your choice. Some impose no-smoking rules, and others won't permit red wine to be served or the presence of children. Make sure to check into all restrictions before signing on the dotted line, no matter how divine the site may be. All that said, here are a couple of my favorite spots in this category:

OXON HILL MANOR

If a water view is on your wish list, Oxon Hill Manor is the place to celebrate. Nestled on the Maryland side of the Potomac River, it can compete with any site in this category in our region. The current Georgian-style structure was built in 1928. The original 1710 house, which was several hundred yards north of today's Manor, once was home to Nathaniel Washington, who cared for family members of George Washington. The original mansion was destroyed by fire in 1895.

Owned and operated by the Maryland-National Capital Park and Planning Commission, the Manor can be rented for social and business events, and at a fairly moderate price. Fees, as usual, vary by day of week and season, with the lowest cost charged to nonprofit groups for weekday events. Oxon Hill Manor is well worth its cost, and it is well worth adhering to its rules. But be sure that you understand all the requirements for service providers, what is prohibited, and what you are responsible for before signing a contract.

Your guests will enter through a magnificent foyer.

To the left is the drawing room, which can be used for dancing. The library, which is straight ahead, is a perfect location for a bar and/or dessert buffet. The dining room is to the right of the library, with a pantry and a kitchen behind it. A beautiful terrace extends across the back of the formal rooms and overlooks the tranquil gardens. Another terrace is off the drawing room. A hallway to the right of the foyer leads to the handicapped entrance and the bridal dressing room. The gardens afford a stunning setting for any type of ceremony, especially a wedding. Tents can be erected, but restrictions apply. The good news about the Manor is that it can accommodate your needs, rain or shine, and that plenty of parking space is available. Located just off Route 495, the Manor will accommodate 300 guests for a standup reception, 210 for a seated lunch or dinner and 170 seated with dancing.

NEWTON WHITE MANSION

You can begin or end your celebration with a gorgeous sunset at the Newton White Mansion. Part of a 600-acre estate in a pastoral setting a few miles from Route 495 in Mitchellville, Maryland, the stately mansion is ideal for wedding ceremonies and receptions and for all types of social and business entertaining. Situated beyond a beautiful courtyard with a circular drive, the mansion was the home of Naval Captain Newton White, who was the first commanding officer of the USS Enterprise, and it, too, is now owned and operated by the Maryland-National Capital Park and Planning Commission.

Rental fees, which are again fairly moderate, are for a seven-hour period, with additional charges for each hour above that. Specific regulations apply to renting this mansion, too, so check on them ahead of time.

Guests enter the Mansion through a main hall, with the study and ballroom to the right. Outside are a patio and a large porch, and a lower patio with a circular fountain is just beyond. All are perfect for ceremonies or for al fresco dining. The dining room and kitchen and a small porch are to the left off the main hall. A large atrium accommodates 250 guests for a seated affair with dancing. The elegant Peach Room, which is perfect for small gatherings, is to the left of the main entry. Tenting is permitted on the garden patio. The upper floor is available for bridal parties. Most events that include ceremonies can be accommodated, rain or shine, and there is ample parking. Overall guest capacity is 300.

COUNTRY INNS

Another charming alternative is to hold your affair in an inn, accommodations that also abound in the region. Here are a couple of my favorites:

THE ELKRIDGE FURNACE INN
Listed on the National Register of Historic Places, the Elkridge Furnace Inn in Elkridge, Maryland, is perfect for wedding ceremonies and receptions,

business meetings, small dinner parties and elegant celebrations of any kind. A gem, the Federal/Greek Revival complex includes the Inn's main structure, the Tavern (circa 1744) and the Manor Home with a Colonial revival porch (circa 1810). Perched on 16 acres in the eastern corner of Howard County, the Inn sits atop the banks of the Patapsco River. It is minutes from BWI Airport and about an hour's drive from Washington, D.C., off Interstate 195.

Food at the Inn can compete with the finest establishments in the Washington region, and at attractive prices. Exclusive catering is provided to the Inn by The Weckers Inc. The menu is conceptually creative and varied, with appetizing and expertly prepared offerings even for the most discerning gourmet. David Carney, who heads the staff, is a talented and creative professional. Charges are calculated according to the number of guests and are relatively moderate and well worth the price. They include food, tax, gratuity, rental, labor, non-alcoholic beverages, china, glassware, flatware, tables,

---

THE MIDDLE WAY:

J.W. Marriott

The J.W. Marriott is a popular choice when it comes to mid-range hotels. It offers a variety of spaces, from a Grand Ballroom (which can accommodate 1,100 for a seated meal or 1,500 for a reception) to small rooms (for 60 or fewer).

On the 12th floor are several suites adjacent to a terrace that affords a panoramic view of the city. One of the two Presidential suites in particular is just right for a small or second wedding, a birthday party, an anniversary celebration or just about any intimate occasion.

The stunning terrace, which can accommodate up to 450 guests, can be used in connection with any of the suites and can even be tented in inclement weather, though doing so will add considerably to the bill.

Many view "The J.W." (as it is affectionately known) as a hotel for conventions or corporate entertaining. It certainly does attract such business. But to Washington-area insiders, it is also known as a good, all-round, moderately priced place to entertain. Importantly, the service is excellent and the food superb.

chairs, dance floor and house-stocked linen. The prices are exclusive of alcohol, dessert and over-time. Specific rules and regulations apply to all events here as well.

Guests enter the Manor Home through a hallway, with a staircase leading to several small to medium-sized rooms above. These upper-level rooms are perfect for intimate dinners for two or for small groups celebrating any special occasion. The rooms also can be used for bridal party dressing rooms. There are two adjacent rooms to the left of the entry hall; the front room can be used for small meetings, or rehearsal dinners, the next room, leading toward the back of the house, for a standup reception or other small gathering. Straight ahead is a kitchen where a small buffet can be served.

Continuing on and down a small flight of stairs, you reach a large, tented patio, an area that can be used in most weather. Parties can extend into the garden behind the tent, and a garden gazebo over-looking the river provides the right touch of romance for a wedding ceremony. Groups of 50 to 200 can be accommodated. Ample parking is available. An added bonus is supplied compliments of the Homewood Suites Hotel at BWI Airport. It will provide shuttle service to and from your event for guests staying overnight at the hotel, where rooms are available at reduced prices.

NOTE: The Tavern serves lunch and dinner daily, so you need not wait until you have a group to entertain. A truly memorable meal awaits you, served by some of the most efficient and friendly staff you'll find anywhere.

THE BAILIWICK INN
The Bailiwick Inn is not in the country. It is an elegant luxury inn in the heart of Old Town in Fairfax, Virginia, across the street from the historic old courthouse. Built sometime between 1800 and 1812 in the Federal style, its bricks were imported from England. In 1861 it was a private home, and the Battle of Fairfax Courthouse took place on its front lawn and resulted in the first Confederate war casualty. The property was home over the years to a succession of commercial tenants and in 1989 was named the Bailiwick Inn.

Whether you are at the Inn for dinner or as a member of a group for a larger celebration or corporate meeting, arriving there is a delight in itself. You are greeted at the door by a butler, who takes your coat, welcomes you and ushers dinner customers into the parlor area. A most efficient and friendly gentlemen, the butler serves drinks from an authentic English pub-type bar, well stocked with your favorite cocktails, and passes tasty hors d'oeuvres. Winter evenings are particularly cozy as you choose your meal from the seasonal menu in front of a delightful, wood-burning fireplace. Drinks done, the butler leads you to the small dinning room at the back of the Inn where you will enjoy a memorable meal, expertly prepared by Chef Jeff Prather, who brings both traditional French and New American flavors to his cuisine.

The Inn has 14 guestrooms. Each is named after a famous Virginian and decorated with period antiques and reproductions.

The entire Inn or parts of it, including all or some of its guestrooms, can be rented for special occasions. Up to 45 guests can be accommodated for a seated buffet or 65 or so for a cocktail reception. Use of the garden facilities will add room for about 10 to 15 more guests, but counting on that space can be dicey if the weather doesn't cooperate. The Inn nonetheless says that it can accommodate 85 for "full house weddings."

Whether you are there for a birthday meal, a meeting, a wedding or any celebration, the Inn staff expertly executes every detail. Prices are not inexpensive, but you can count on a memorable experience.   ◆

CHAPTER II

Entertaining at Home

*That which chiefly causes the failure of a dinner party, is the
running short—not of meat, nor yet of drink, but of conversation.*

—LEWIS CARROLL

SOME PEOPLE PREFER to entertain at home, even if it means tackling a wedding, a bar or bat mitzvah or another big affair there. This isn't because holding a large celebration in your house is likely to cut expenses, as those who have seen *The Father of the Bride* should know well. You still will incur the costs of vendors examined elsewhere in this book— caterer, baker, musicians, photographers, florist, party planner, providers of invitations, tents (essential unless all guests can fit comfortably inside), tables, chairs, china, linens, silverware and other equipment. Those who hold large-scale celebrations at home generally do so because of the personal meaning it adds to the affair, not to cut budgets.

Most of us, however, tend to do more modest and less formal entertaining in our homes —dinner, cocktail, birthday or retirement parties, showers, New Year's Eve, July 4th and other holiday gatherings, Super Bowl bashes, political fundraisers, parties honoring or introducing special people or visiting friends, get-togethers of neighbors, colleagues, discussion groups and contributors to charitable causes. *(See box on p. 20.)* The essential ingredients for such gatherings include a nifty reason, good food and, above all, great guests. Add a dash of sim-

ple elegance, mix with a little creativity, and you've got the prescription for a wonderful party—and one that doesn't have to break the bank.

An invitation to your home is the highest compliment you can pay someone, and most guests are happy just to be there, so resist any urge to go overboard. Keeping things as simple as possible, and knowing your strengths and weaknesses, can turn an ordinary occasion into a memorable one.

THE OCCASION

Last-minute get-togethers are often great fun, but it generally is preferable to invite guests for a special occasion that you have planned in advance. Perhaps the most popular form of home entertaining is the dinner party, which can satisfy various purposes, but there are many other approaches as well. While it would be impossible to list them all here, consider a handful of examples:

◆ **"SUNSET SIPS."** Cocktail parties are popular, I think, because guests enjoy the informality of mingling with lots of people and the ease of a buffet and passed hors d'oeuvres, not to mention a flexible time commitment. But an invitation for cocktails suggests the same old thing. To add a special touch, you can instead invite people for, say, "A Sunset Sip." Sunsets always generate excitement. On Greece's Santorini Island, for instance, I watched devotees gather on the terraces of little bars perched atop tall cliffs to watch one of nature's great gifts. At first there was absolute silence—followed by thunderous applause as the golden ball dipped below the horizon. Half a world away, the celebration is replicated nightly as tourists and residents alike gather on Mallory Square in Key West, Florida.

Obviously, you can't guarantee a fabulous sunset for your guests—but you can rent one. Just pick up a video with sunsets at your local rental establishment or from the tourist bureau of some tropical paradise. Dim the lights and put the video on a continuous loop on your VCR.

Voilà—a perfect sunset to accompany your potables, and your guests can marvel at the performance more than once!

◆ **AFTERNOON TEAS.** Sunday afternoons are convenient for guests and hosts alike to take time from their hectic schedules to spend time with friends, neighbors and associates. Afternoon tea is a lovely way to entertain at home for a variety of reasons. A tea offers the flexibility of a cocktail party but somehow suggests a more relaxed atmosphere. It also offers the economy of hosting an event during non-meal hours. You can include alcoholic beverages, such as champagne, wine or sherry, if you wish. Little sandwiches, tiny cakes, sweets and pots of tea round out an inexpensive menu that is easy to prepare.

◆ **SUNDAY SUPPERS.** Sunday evening is also a relaxing time. Gathering a group of family, colleagues,

Charity Indeed Begins at Home

Some people like to entertain in their homes to raise money for a charitable organization. Others like to do it in the community—say, through a pool party or a street party, both fun ways to have a good time while helping a good cause and setting a good example for the young.

Julie Hanson, of the public relations firm Susan Davis International, who handles high-level fundraising benefits, says, "These events have a way of growing and becoming a family or neighborhood tradition, some getting media attention and raising lots of money." For anyone interested, she suggests starting small, but she also stresses the need to keep looking for ways to grow the event.

Judy Whittlesey, executive vice president of the firm, adds that building a solid budget and sticking to it is crucial to the success of such affairs. "It's important . . . to carefully consider what you absolutely cannot cut and what you can live without," she says.

I agree—and I cannot think of a better way to celebrate.

book club members or others for supper enables the host to set an informal table with simple food and to do so early enough for everyone to be back home at a reasonable hour—in time to be refreshed for work Monday morning.

- ◆ **GARDEN PARTIES.** Chip Knight, a public relations executive, says, "If you've worked really hard re-landscaping your garden and it's in full bloom, the green thumbs in your social circle would probably really enjoy seeing it." Hence a garden party or patio barbecue to show it off (together with an explanation of your planting plans) could be great fun.

THE MENU

Some of the wealthy among us have personal chefs to prepare gourmet feasts when they entertain at home. Others plan and prepare their own elegant meals for sit-down or buffet lunches or dinners. Still others have caterers provide the food or order in from various restaurants. But the food you serve need not be complicated and costly. It can be simple and inexpensive, so long as it is fresh, tasty, plentiful and presented well. For a brunch, for example, you can pick up varieties of smoked fish and bagels from the store and add your own fritatas. For a great buf-fet lunch—especially for a Super Bowl or Kentucky Derby party or other casual get-together—you can serve really good hot dogs on fresh rolls. Put out toppings like New York-style onions in tomato sauce or sauerkraut or three-alarm chili (mild for the meek), grated ched-dar cheese, relish and a variety of mustards. Place everything in fun serving pieces, add tubs of beer, wine, soft drinks and waters, sprinkle the house with pots of daisies or other seasonal flowers and you've got an economi-cal scenario for a wonderful party.

One-dish meals that can be prepared in advance are also great choices and will help to keep you out of

Per-Person Minimums

Allow the following amounts of food and beverages for each guest:

HORS D'OEUVRES	5 to 6 pieces per 1/2 hour reception
BUFFET ITEMS	1/4 lb. per item, i.e., shrimp, carved meat, etc.
OPEN BAR	1.5 drinks per hour*
DINNER WINE	1/2 bottle **

One 32-ounce bottle of liquor will serve about 21 drinks of 1 1/2 ounces each.

** *One 7.5-ml. bottle will serve 5/6 glasses. Have at least two drinking/wine glasses for each guest.*

the kitchen, particularly if you are doing the cook-ing. They can be economical, too, and fall into the comfort-food category. One-dish meals also offer the luxury of keeping warm in the oven while you and your guests enjoy the first course. Obviously stews, pot pies or Italian delights such as Lasagna come to mind, but cold dishes like Salad Niçoise can be creatively presented on one beautiful platter from which guests can be served.

For more formal occasions, multi-course meals also can be relatively easy and yet ele-gant. Start with pâté and champagne or sparkling water or cider. One well-known Washington host-ess likes to serve hot, crispy bacon as an hors d'oeu-vre, and guests love it. Other crowd pleasers, especially served with champagne, are chunks of Parmesan cheese. Follow that with simply grilled fish, poultry or meat, marinated vegetables and salad. Pass crusty bread and grizzini, and offer a choice of red or white wine. Pick a decadent dessert like gooey chocolate cake or go as light as orange slices and sorbet, along with coffee and liqueurs.

Less formal meals might include meatloaf and mashed potatoes. Two of my closest friends adore this meal, which they say reminds them of their childhoods. It's a perfect menu for a winter Sunday supper, one that, for some, will warm not only the stomach but also the soul.

Don't hesitate to serve such meals, moreover, on different china. It's not always necessary to present food on the same pattern for each course or even for the same course, for that matter. Mixing china and glassware can be quite attractive, a conversation starter and lots of fun.

If you want to let your hair down with really good friends, hire a Chinese chef! All you have to do is serve something to nosh with drinks and put the finishing touches on dessert while guests are selecting what they want for dinner from the local Chinese restaurant carry-out menu. One phone call later, everyone is enjoying his or her favorite Chinese meal. It's so enjoyable, so easy and so relaxing.

In all this, you should, of course, keep in mind the special needs of some guests, making sure, for example, that sufficient salad and pasta are available for vegetarians and that meals are designed for elderly guests as well as for the young. In addition, it is important to remember not to keep guests waiting to eat. If you are serving a buffet, be sure the food is placed on the table before guests arrive.

If a seated meal is planned, serve drinks for no longer than 30 to 40 minutes before dinner.

THE GUESTS

As Lewis Carroll noted, dinner parties do not fail because they run short of food or drink but because of a scarcity of good conversation. That is perhaps what once prompted British journalist Simon Hoggart to remark: "The formal Washington dinner party has all the spontaneity of a Japanese imperial funeral." Obviously, the key to avoiding such scripted rigidity, whether during formal or informal entertaining at home, is to be blessed with interesting and warm guests.

As Liz Hylton, longtime personal assistant to the late Katharine Graham, the legendary chairman and chief executive of The Washington Post Company, said, "Pay special attention to the guest list. Mix people up, and be sure everyone meets those they don't know." In Mrs. Graham's case, of course, dinner guests often included, in addition to family and friends, Presidents and First Ladies, Prime Ministers, royalty, corporate chieftains, artists, journalists, generals, intellectual lights and others who were not known as wallflowers or as lacking in conversational arts.

But Washington is filled with interesting and warm people from all walks of life, so the task is to make sure that they engage each other. In this regard, one can get helpful counsel from someone like Nancy Chistolini, Senior Vice President, Fashion and Public Relations, at Hecht's, who uses creative ways to ensure that her guests mingle. At one party she hosted, for example, each guest was greeted with an inexpensive, one-size-fits-all beaded bracelet with a tag inscribed with the word "friendship" in different languages. Each tag had a mate, and guests were encouraged to seek their partners. When they finally connected, the newly acquainted duo received a prize. There wasn't one stranger in the room by the time people were seated for dinner.

A gesture like that is not only a wonderful ice-breaker, often relaxing even the shyest person, but it provides mementos to remember the occasion. It can also help ensure that there is no disconnect between guests who are family and those who are friends. One friend of mine, for example, was concerned about melding college-age bridesmaids and her elderly aunts attending a shower that she was hosting for a niece. With a variation of the beaded bracelet, she borrowed the butterfly theme of her niece's wedding decorations. Little cards, adorned with butterfly stickers and inscribed with appropriate wedding-related words in duplicate, "broke the ice, beautifully," she said. "I knew the cards did the trick immediately. There was total chatter in the room." Obviously, many other variations on the bracelets and butterflies can be used, tailored to your particular gathering.

If you hold a celebration at home—say, an engagement party for a friend—that includes many guests, you also might ask some friends to help make introductions. If a receiving line is in place, arrange for a few people to be available at the end of the line (but no one from the line) who can introduce arriving guests to some of those already congregated. That will make them feel welcome and more comfortable and help get the party going.

It is no secret, of course, that seating arrangements also can do much to induce conversations. With seated meals, hosts and hostesses sometimes have an array of reasons to pair people. They may want to spark political discussions. They may want to play cupid for unattached friends. They may want to trigger professional exchanges or alliances within or across organizations, and they certainly want to avoid seating shy guests with overbearing ones. It takes some effort to think through how the chem-istry among guests might work, but it is likely to be well worth it in the end.

Whatever pairings you choose, you should make sure guests know where to sit, whether with standard place cards or other devices. Inscribed rocks symbolizing the Blarney Stone, for example, are festive and apropos at a St. Patrick's Day dinner. For many occasions you can use color-coding, coins or picture frames, writing guests' names in the picture space. Guests also can be given cocktail napkins to match their table napkin, a shiny silver dollar or a tiny statue of Mickey Mouse or another notable character, with instructions to locate the mate at the table.

It is also important for you to avoid certain actions and attitudes that can sour things for your guests and for your affair. Here are some of them:

◆ **MONOPOLIZING THE GUEST OF HONOR.** If there is a guest of honor, be careful not to monopolize or isolate that person. One unfortunate tale I know of involved a close friend who was invited to the retirement party of a New York co-worker. After flying from Washington at her own expense to attend, she found it impossible to get near the guest of honor, whom the host kept in virtual captivity for the entire evening. My friend was terribly hurt. What should have been a delightful evening was ruined because the host failed to consider and involve every guest.

◆ **DEALING POORLY WITH UNEXPECTED GUESTS.** It is not unheard of for a guest to ask someone else to tag along—which sometimes can result in embarrassment for all. For example, because of an incorrect assumption (assuming anything is a cardinal sin in entertaining as in all else), an invited guest asked a friend to accompany him to a party for another mutual friend. The tag-along guest agreed, but only to stop by, say hello to the guest of honor and leave. The hosts assumed (there's that word again) that the unexpected guest intended to stay for dinner and informed her, within earshot of others, that there was no room.

That resulted in hurt feelings all around, which easily could have been avoided. The guest who did the inviting should have asked the hosts beforehand. The hosts, albeit panicked, simply should have said how pleased they were to have the additional guest for dinner and tried to work things out. Had that happened, the woman would have thanked them but declined, as she had intended all along, and things would have gone well for everybody.

◆ **KEEPING PEOPLE IN THE DARK.** Another embarrassing case of incorrect assumptions involved a friend who has for years been invited to a particular party given by good friends. The annual gathering had always been a buffet, with guests coming and going according to their own schedules. Assuming the status quo, my friend arrived almost an hour after the starting time on the invitation. However, this year the hosts had decided on a seated dinner—without indicating the change on the invitation. My friend arrived to find a group of hungry guests awaiting her. Of course, the hosts incorrectly assumed that everyone would arrive at, roughly, the same time. The lesson: It is essential for guests to know what they are invited for, so be sure to include all the details on your invitation, in plain words that everyone can understand (including what type of dress is appropriate). This should be done whether you send a formal invitation or invite close friends by phone or e-mail.

The Gracious Guest

Your hosts are as deserving of your thoughtfulness as you are of theirs. If you want to be a gracious guest, take note:

◆ Always arrive on time for a seated meal. A grace period of 15 minutes is acceptable. After that you will put your host's schedule in jeopardy.

◆ Inform your host of any dietary restrictions or allergies, including ones to animals, well ahead of time. Don't wait until you arrive to divulge your sensitivities.

◆ You can bring candy, wine or a small gift, but don't expect the food or beverages to be served at the gathering unless you were specifically asked to bring something.

◆ If you wish to give flowers, send them to the host's home, after the event along with a thank you note, rather than bring them with you. That way the host does not have the extra chore of arranging them at the time of the event.

◆ Don't come for drinks but not stay for dinner. It's impolite to do so except under the most unusual circumstances, and it will complicate matters for the host.

◆ Don't monopolize conversation. It's far better to encourage others to take part in the discussion even if they seem reluctant to do so.

◆ Don't get too comfortable. It's embarrassing to overstay one's welcome.

◆ Don't expect the host to arrange to get you home unless it is so stated in the invitation. If you are not driving, prearrange for a taxi pickup.

DON'T GET LOST IN THE KITCHEN

For the sake of both you and your guests, you need to find ways to stay out of the kitchen when you are entertaining at home. There's nothing worse than an absent hostess. If too much cooking and serving consume your time, it will be impossible for you to be gracious and for guests to enjoy your company, let alone for you to have a good time, as you surely should. It is important, therefore, to leave room in your budget to hire help or, at a minimum, for someone to help you serve and clean up.

If these are not options, or if you are determined to show off your culinary skills, you should coordinate beforehand with your spouse or a close friend so that one of you is always with guests, making sure that the conversation keeps going and attending to their needs. Children or grandchildren make good candidates for duty as well. My adolescent grandson loves to pass hors d'oeuvres and bring platters and serving dishes to the table, and he is quite good at it. My eldest granddaughter loves to light the table candles and is happy to clear dishes. While you may not want to press them into service in all cases, it can be fun to have young family members at the very least greet guests and take coats. You'll be surprised at how much more time you can spend with guests by designating even such minor chores.

Remember that, at seated meals especially, you can make all the difference in keeping those discussions going. Indeed, you should make sure that everyone is engaged in the conversations. It is polite, for example, for you to speak first to the guest on your right. After a reasonable period, you should then address the person on your left, letting the guest on your right converse with the guest on his or her right and so on. This works particularly well at a round table. Conversation with guests at the opposite end of a rectangular table, though, is obviously more difficult. Therefore, it is a good idea for the hosts, who usually sit at either end of a rectangular table, to exchange places at some point, generally after dessert is served. This allows them to talk with everyone. It is a subtle gesture but a gracious one that will help make all of your guests feel welcome.

If guests are seated at more than one table, host and hostess certainly should make the rounds to ensure that all is going well. Liz Hylton adds that you also can make guests feel more welcome if you put a table where they least expect it, in the living room, for instance, or on a balcony, patio or deck. A meal served on lap trays in the family room is another way to make friends feel cozy and more at home in your home. ◆

CHAPTER III

Heading for Exotic Spots

Far away places with strange-soundin' names
Far away over the sea
Those far away places with the strange-soundin' names
Are callin', callin' me

— ALEX KRAMER AND JOAN WHITNEY
Far Away Places

YOU CAN DO IT on a beach. You can do it on a ship. You can even do it while diving from a plane or swimming underwater. The ways to hold your celebrations are legion, and traditional affairs, particularly weddings, are being challenged by many exotic variations, both abroad and domestically.

While milestone birthdays and anniversaries, renewals of vows, reunions and other events can be celebrated in unorthodox places and ways, the most popular non-traditional alternative is the "destination wedding," defined simply by where it's held. That can be just about anywhere. If you've always wanted to be married in a castle à la Cinderella or in the town square of a French village, it certainly can be arranged. All you need is imagination and an understanding of the advantages, disadvantages and special requirements involved.

While marriages performed outside the country are recognized as legal, for example, it's essential to know the marriage license requirements of the nation (or the state or other jurisdiction) where you plan to wed—and to take nothing for granted. One couple I know of who wanted to wed on the Caribbean island of St. Lucia found this out the hard way. They had planned a videotaped fairytale ceremony on the beach at a leading hotel. After the wedding and honeymoon, they were to return home to a lovely reception, given by the bride's parents, at which the video of the wedding ceremony

was to be shown. But disaster struck on the wedding day: The couple was unaware of a St. Lucia residence and waiting requirement—and the registrar refused to marry them. Heartbroken, the bride couldn't imagine what she would tell her mother.

Fortunately, there was a happy ending. A wonderful group of hotel guests proposed a mock wedding, and the desperate couple agreed. The pretend minister, Neil Turnbull of Lancashire, England, who orchestrated the entire scheme, donned a white-collared shirt worn backwards beneath a waiter's black jacket. A covered beach novel served as The Good Book, from which the imposter read invented vows, and the guests cheered as he pronounced the couple husband and wife. The couple went home, and the celebration proceeded as planned. The "minister" received a note from the couple a few months later: "No one was the wiser. We made it legal right before the reception."

You will be wiser, however, if you get everything in order in advance, including backup plans in case of bad weather. Remember that it can rain for long periods in the tropics, as it did for one couple I know of who planned a beach wedding at sunset. When ceremony time arrived, a menacing sky and strong winds were unraveling nerves and hairdos. Yet hotel personnel kept setting tables under a parawing tent (beautiful for decoration, ridiculous for shelter) and arranging guest chairs on the beach. After a lengthy delay, the rain subsided and the beach ceremony took place despite wet chairs and a fine mist. The reception didn't fare as well: The buffet dinner had to be held in the hotel lobby, amid the comings and goings of curious hotel guests. No matter how beautiful the site, if you can't move inside to a previously selected backup location, you could be courting disaster. *(See Partying Under a Tent, p. 67.)*

WEIGHING THE PROS AND CONS

Some couples choose to marry where they met, where they spent a romantic interlude or where they have always dreamed of going. Others want celebrations built around favorite activities like skiing or mountain climbing. Still others pick a destination wedding for other reasons—some, for example, for a second marriage, others because family conflicts make a traditional wedding at home too painful or impossible. Whatever your reason might be, you should ponder some of the pluses and minuses involved:

♦ **FEWER GUESTS.** Because of travel expenses, destination weddings tend to be smaller than those held at home. Thus some people you might very much want at your wedding might not be able to attend.

♦ **LOWER COSTS.** Obviously, having fewer guests also keeps down expenses. So does the fact that fewer decorations, and even flowers, are necessary when the setting provides its own special décor. You also have the option, like the St. Lucia couple, of returning home for a celebration party that can be just that—a party, which is a lot cheaper than a wedding reception with all the trimmings. (When guests do accompany them, some couples find that the lower expenses leave room in the budget for them to provide golf greens fees or to organize some other activity.)

♦ **TRANSPORTATION AND LODGING ETIQUETTE.** Most couples who pick destination weddings don't pay

for guest transportation and lodging but do provide some meals. As with traditional weddings, it's common for out-of-town guests—meaning virtually everybody in this case—to be invited to a rehearsal dinner and a day-after brunch. Some etiquette gurus consider it inappropriate to ask guests to foot bills for transportation, lodging and some meals to attend a wedding at a distant spot they may never have wanted to visit. But many out-of-towners at traditional weddings do the same thing already, and many guests view destination weddings not only as an opportunity to share a special occasion with family and friends but to turn it into a vacation as well.

♦ **JUST THE TWO OF YOU.** If you choose to return home for a party, you should be sure that you can handle the solitude of marrying by yourselves. It is not always a cheerful sight for two people to pledge their lives to one another before strangers who act as officiant and witnesses and under the gaping eyes of passersby and onlookers. I can remember witnessing one such wedding. Champagne and cake were served after the ceremony in full view of the same onlookers, and there was a terrible awkwardness that followed as bride and groom walked away with seemingly nowhere to go.

♦ **A TOLERANCE FOR THE UNKNOWN.** Unless you have already been to your version of paradise, you will have to pick a venue sight unseen. Are you willing to do that? (While the Internet can depict various views of sites, that certainly is not the same as seeing them in person.) You also will have to trust important decisions to someone you have never met. Just about anywhere you choose will provide the services of an on-site employee to help you. On the plus side, this will significantly reduce the details and stress that you otherwise would have to deal with yourself. But you have to be comfortable working with someone long distance.

If you work directly with an employee of the

establishment you have chosen, be sure that he or she has experience with weddings and that coordinating your event is his or her main responsibility. If you have any doubts about the person to whom you have been assigned, it is well worth the expense to hire a wedding coordinator familiar with the place and facility you've chosen (they generally can be found online or can be recommended by the hotel).

◆ **EARLY NOTICE, HOTELS AND AIRLINES.** Destination weddings generally require longer notice than traditional weddings, so announcements to guests should be sent at least six months in advance. It is also a good idea to reserve a block of hotel rooms and even airline seats, if possible. Hotels will be happy to work with you, particularly if both the ceremony and reception are held at their hotel.

Check with airlines directly for group-reservations information.

An away-from-home wedding or other celebration is a big step, but if you know what you want and can celebrate the event with family and friends, even if after returning home, it can be a wonderful alternative.

A SAFARI, A BEACH OR A CRUISE SHIP?

Would you like to marry or celebrate the milestones in your life on an African safari? On a mountaintop? Among giant redwoods? While skydiving or scuba diving? There is virtually no limit to the kind of experience you can choose. *(See boxes on pp. 28, 30 and 31.)* For weddings, however, the hottest spots tend to be on or near beaches at sun-

---

Marriage in Mid-Air

According to the United States Parachuting Association, many couples across the nation who are licensed skydivers choose the exhilaration of free-fall weddings, and parachute enthusiasts in the Washington region certainly can join in the jumping affairs.

Interested parties can contact such outfits as Skydive Orange, in Fisherville, Virginia, or The Sky Diving Center, in Ocean City, Maryland.

Some parachutists choose to take vows in mid-air. In that case, after you jump, 60 to 70 seconds lapse before you pull the chute, followed by a guided four to six minutes to the ground. The officiant who jumps with you usually motions to nod on cue at the traditional "I do" part of the ceremony. Ear devices or cellular devices are available, through which all three

can communicate, but they are not guaranteed to operate properly in the air. Couples should also be aware that bad weather could ground the wedding.

Other parachutists choose to marry on the ground before going up to skydive, and some take their vows in the plane before jumping.

Skydive Orange says that it is happy to accommodate weddings, though the couple is responsible for arranging whatever ceremony they prefer and what happens before or after the jump. The Sky Diving Center warns that bridal attire can be problematic. Divers can jump in just about anything, and custom-made wedding diving suits can be made at considerable cost, but a traditional wedding dress will need preapproval.

set. Cruise ships are running a close second. Since it is impossible to examine every potential destination, let's focus mainly on those popular options.

ON U.S. TERRITORY

For beaches, the U.S. Virgin Islands and Puerto Rico, both under the U.S. flag, are hard to beat and easy to reach. They are served by major airlines, with flights from all three Washington-area airports. Both have destination management companies and on-site personnel who can assist with all aspects of planning and executing your celebration.

Take St. Thomas. The Ritz Carlton there, overlooking Great Bay on the trendy east end of the island, is exceptional. The hotel, which is reminiscent of an Italian palazzo, is on an extraordinary site with panoramic views. You can be married or renew your vows on the beach at sunset, in front of a stand of graceful sea grapes, or on either of two outdoor terraces perched high above the sea. An intimate interior courtyard and several lush gardens are also available for ceremonies. Related events can be held at the seaside pool bar, in a section of the fine dining room, or in either of two palatial ballrooms. The Marriott Frenchmen's Reef, near town, can accommodate large and small groups, as can its adjoining sister property, the very lovely Morning Star Beach Resort.

Indeed, choices are plentiful on many islands, whether for grand affairs or smaller ones. Another St. Thomas spot for large celebrations is St. Peter Greathouse Estate and Gardens, an 11-acre, hillside site on the island's north side with breathtaking views and elegant facilities and grounds. For more intimate celebrations, one might turn to The Relais & Chateau Horned Dorset Primavera in Rincon, Puerto Rico. Likened by *Washington Post* travel writer Gary Lee to Virginia's Inn at Little Washington, this is a smaller, secluded hotel on the ocean with no phones or TVs. Its grounds and elegant surroundings are second only to its restaurant, where meals are superb.

If you wish to remain in the United States but travel further from Washington, Hawaii has long been a popular destination. It is famous for weddings held at the Blue Grotto in Honolulu, which is particularly favored by couples from Japan. Every Hawaiian island, though, has beautiful hotels for your dream day, one in particular being the Hyatt Hotel on Maui.

ABOARD A SHIP

Most cruise lines offer wedding packages and have wedding coordinators available to plan and execute a ceremony and, if you choose, a reception. A few will refer you to an independent planner to make the arrangements.

All lines require you to book passage first. They want to be sure they can accommodate you on your sailing date before making the wedding arrangements. Newer and larger cruise ships have wedding chapels, but older and smaller ones without chapels reserve the right to decide where your ceremony will be held. You may request a specific location, but it will depend on the size of your party and whether other couples are getting married on the same day. (Floor plans of the ship usually are available on the cruise line's web site, but they are not going to tell you everything you need to know.) Ship captains today generally do not have the power to perform a legal marriage. Most ships, though, have a cleric on board. If religious denomination is a factor, however, you may have to make special arrangements for someone of your faith to perform the ceremony.

On-board receptions usually are quite reasonably priced, whether for a sit-down lunch or a stand-up reception. Naturally, cruise lines hope that your guests will sail away with you, netting them the cruise fare, but that may depend on the port of departure for the cruise. If guests are flying from Washington to Miami or San Juan, some might take that as an opportunity to vacation a bit in Florida or Puerto Rico, letting the newlyweds sail off by themselves. Others might join the cruise, especially if they've never been on one.

Some couples, on the other hand, view the ship as a vacation spot—as transportation to another place (perhaps one of those pristine Caribbean beaches) where they want to be married. Couples can arrange to be met at the dock, transported to the ceremony site and even to a reception, where they and their guests can celebrate appropriately. Just about anything is possible, but how much you can fit in will depend on how long the ship will be in port.

SOME OTHER CHOICES

There are, of course, many other choices for destination weddings and other celebrations, whether on different beaches or inland. For example:

BERMUDA. If you do not want to travel far, Bermuda, which is popular with wedding couples, is little more than an hour flight from the Washington area. On that lovely Atlantic island off the Carolinas you will find, for example, the Pink Beach Club and Cottages, a moderately priced hotel with a pleasant atmosphere, exceptional service and ceremonies on the beach at sunset that are said to be stunning. The hotel offers a wedding package to handle all arrangements, including the necessary paperwork and requirements for a Bermuda marriage license.

LAS VEGAS. Las Vegas is famous for wedding chapels and the absence of a waiting period, so hastily planned nuptials can take place. Every Las Vegas hotel has a wedding package, with little difference among them. Most offer use of the hotel wedding

Watery Weddings

If an underwater wedding is your idea of bliss, the Florida Keys provide some fine spots, as do various Caribbean islands.

Kelly's on the Bay in Key Largo, Florida, for example, is adept at watery weddings, handling items ranging from the ceremony, the videography and still photography to bridal bouquets, grooms' boutonnieres and communications systems—all water friendly. According to Jamie Houck of Kelly's, bouquets are made to withstand the dive.

Houck says that the ceremony begins when the couple, wedding party and officiant take their places underwater. The bride and groom pledge their devotion by using slates that already have the vows (personalized if you wish) printed on them. The couple can nod, sign "I do" or speak

the words through the underwater communications system.

Attire for the ceremony is usually quite innovative, and couples like to get involved in designing their duds. Many brides opt for a white bathing suit and then add personal touches, from trains and frilly skirts to veils. Wet suits can also be designed for the couple if they wish, and some grooms select tuxedo-like suits.

What Kelly's doesn't handle is the catering, says Houck, but it can recommend caterers for a celebration on its sundeck/dock area.

The U.S. Virgin Islands also provide good choices for underwater affairs. On St. Thomas, for example, the Ritz Carlton Sports Center offers help with watery weddings.

chapel, flowers, a photography package, champagne and the like, all perfect for last-minute weddings. Of course, you can also plan a more traditional wedding or other celebration in Las Vegas at any one of a number of fairytale places. In either case, the affairs might well lure guests who want to stay to gamble or see popular entertainers and lavish shows.

WINE COUNTRY. Others might want to head for lovely wine country areas. Meadowood, for example, is an elegant Relais & Chateau retreat in St. Helena, California, amid the beauty of the Napa Valley. Self-described as an estate that lends itself to an elegant evening wedding ceremony in summer, a fireside exchange of vows in winter, or a family reunion or other celebrations, the hotel offers a wide selection of accommodations, fine dining and activities for guests. Closer to home, in the emerging wine country of Virginia, the Oasis Vineyard can accommodate large and small celebrations, including weddings. The vineyard itself has no lodging accommodations, but guests can stay at any number of nearby historic inns and bed-and-breakfasts.

ALL-INCLUSIVE PROPERTIES. Another good alternative is all-inclusive properties. You can still combine the wedding and the honeymoon, but there are no time constraints, and you can usually choose the site you prefer for your ceremony. Some of the best are in St. Lucia, Antigua, Hawaii, the Bahamas, Mexico and the continental United States. On St. Lucia, for instance, Rendezvous, just outside of the capital of Castries, is a mid-priced, couples-only resort that offers a variety of wedding packages. LeSport, owned by the same family, is a more upscale resort that also includes a spa and offers accommodations for the entire family.

RENTED VILLAS. The U.S. and British Virgin Islands, Barbados, St. Barths and Jamaica are noted for luxurious villas that can be rented, with staff available to tidy up, do laundry and prepare meals. Renting a large villa is one idea gaining popularity among families celebrating milestone birthdays or planning reunions.

The list can go on almost endlessly, as can the joy and memories of such celebrations. ◆

Nuptials for the Cave People

If you are a lover—of caves filled with stalactite and stalagmite, that is—you can hold your wedding at Luray Caverns in Luray, Virginia, joining more than 300 other couples who have been married there since the caverns opened to tourists in 1878.

"Although the weddings used to be a novelty that got a lot of publicity, they are a money-making operation now," John Shaffer, Luray Caverns public relations director, said, adding that the cave nuptials are held "about five to six times a season."

The evening ceremony usually takes place in the Cathedral Room, which has the most available floor space and which also holds the Great Stalacpipe Organ, whose keys electronically prompt rubber-tipped mallets to tap stalactites in the 3 1/2 acres of caverns.

Up to 50 guests get a tour of the caverns as they are escorted to the Cathedral Room. Receptions are sometimes held in the caverns' restaurant, but other Luray venues can be chosen.

CHAPTER IV

The Best Laid Plans

(Are the Ones You Hire Someone Else to Handle)

*Plans are only good intentions unless
they immediately degenerate into hard work.*

— PETER F. DRUCKER

ANYONE PLANNING a sizable bash, whether for a wedding, a milestone birthday, a reunion or another occasion, will soon find the task daunting. As this book makes clear, the elements are many, the decisions seemingly endless and the possible mishaps plentiful, not only in the period leading up to the event but at the affair itself. The last thing you want is a celebration filled with foul-ups. The next-to-last thing you want is to be overcharged for it.

There is one step you can take to avoid such pitfalls: Hire an event planner. Mame Reilly, formerly of Washington, Inc., says, "You may think you can't afford to hire a planner. In reality you can't afford *not* to." In the end, in fact, the planner may well save you money, and she or he definitely can save you lots of time and stress before and during the affair. In other words, the planner can make the difference between whether the memories of your celebration will be of joy or grief.

As with other service providers, event planners abound in the Washington area, and most are affiliated with some professional organization—the International Special Events Society, the National Association of Catering Executives or the Association of Wedding Professionals. Some concentrate on weddings and others on corporate or government clients, but most do both. Weddings and corporate events "are two different animals," says Linda Garner of Gala Events. "A wedding is very personal and you become emotionally involved, sometimes making lifetime friends. When you work with a corporation, you concentrate mainly on executing a set program with a certain budget. But the skills required are the same."

So is the route for finding the planner for you: getting recommendations from friends, family and colleagues and checking with caterers, hotel catering directors and venue representatives. Look for a planner whose taste is compatible with yours, who is not condescending, who knows how to make creative tradeoffs and who is energetic; stamina alone will count for much on the day of your celebration. If possible, when you've narrowed your choices, ask someone who does a fair amount of entertaining to evaluate the credentials of those on your short list.

A good planner will make significant contributions in the following ways:

1. SAVING TIME/REDUCING STRESS
Experienced event planners are well connected and can quickly identify service providers with whom you are likely to work best and who are within your budget range. Relying on such expertise will greatly reduce time-consuming and stressful searches for service providers to help produce your affair. That makes planners particularly attractive to those with hectic lives.

"I have a demanding, high-stress job. I don't have the time." So states Adrian Cotton, who says that the best decision she made about her wedding was to hire Jodi Moraru & Associates. Sara Franco of Romantic Betrothal seconds the customer profile, stating that today's clients are "cool women with hot jobs." (In fact, however, they are not all women. Men increasingly are involved in planning every aspect of events, especially weddings.)

Those without high-stress jobs, however, are likely to appreciate planners as well. When conflicts emerge in orchestrating a wedding—whether over guest lists, seating, expenses or whatever—having a trusted planner to act as a liaison and counselor between dueling parties is invaluable. Should some guests try to switch their place card to a table or seat they prefer, having someone who can quietly handle such awkward moments is worth every penny of the planner's fee. When you are feeling exasperated by all the details of your celebration, having a planner who can get you organized within a short time—and someone who can make sure your plans are not too complicated and are appropriate for the occasion—is a godsend.

This does not mean, of course, that having an event planner guarantees that every potential misstep will be avoided. Don't forget that, as Murphy's law states, anything that can go wrong, will. Remember also that, as a Murphy corollary puts it, if everything seems to be going well, you obviously have overlooked something. The odds are simply stacked against you, and event planners are only human (they cannot, for example, change the fact that, as another Murphy variation states, the other line is always shorter). Generally, however, they are your best line of defense. They are seasoned in navigating around problems with the grace of a gazelle and the finesse of a diplomat.

2. CUTTING COSTS

The best planners know where to find bargains and shave costs. One bride I interviewed for this book happily recounted that what the planner had saved her on her wedding dress almost covered the planner's fee. In many instances, planners not only can negotiate the best prices—they also can turn on a dime. Another bride, who announced to a hotel catering executive that she wanted to be married in six days, not only had the wedding of her dreams but got it for the amount she wanted to pay, thanks to the well-connected and seasoned planner.

Okay, another Murphy's variation holds that no matter how long or how hard you shop for something, after you've bought it, it will be available somewhere cheaper. You can't blame an event planner for that or for the fact that all of us want more than our purses permit. Remember that you control the budget. Carol Millman of A Perfect Wedding says, for example, that her company offers clients cost-saving tips on every aspect of a wedding but that the choices are the customer's to make. "We ask them to prioritize, tell us what's most important to them," she says. "We develop a budget from there."

Developing your budget—and sticking to it—probably is the most important part of any event. It's easy to get off course, ordering this and adding that. Are you sure you really want those monogrammed cocktail napkins? Planners will keep you on track and make recommendations based on what you have told them you can afford. They are also familiar with contracts and can spy trouble spots not always visible to the layperson. It's not hard to accumulate overtime charges for a variety of services, from catering staff to photographers. In the gaiety of the moment, you may be tempted to authorize keeping the bar open or extending the music for an additional hour, which can add sizable chunks to your bill. Not properly calculating setup and

One-Stop Planning

Whether for a wedding, a milestone anniversary or another special occasion, some people want not only the help of a planner but everything related to the event based at a single operation as well. Well, look no further than Occoquan, Virginia, a charming hamlet on the banks of the Occoquan River, or Hunt Country Celebrations, in Fauquier County, Virginia.

In little Occoquan you can get custom-designed rings at Quinn's Goldsmith, invitations at Hawthorne House and a cake at the Garden Kitchen. You can be married in the historic Town Hall, in a small riverside gazebo or at the hillside Rockledge Mansion, circa 1758. Receptions can be held at all these spots as well as at, say, the Occoquan Inn or Sea, Sea & Company. Flowers can be had from Accolades, attendant gifts from Elements and at Allegra's Bridal you will find what owner Susan Ettenson calls "a one-stop shopping experience."

In addition to carrying many designer bridal creations, Allegra's will create dresses for bride and bridal party according to your specifications, or it will alter a wedding gown not purchased there. Grooms can be outfitted in designer tuxedos, and parents can find attire here as well. Brides can get headpieces and veils (specially designed if you wish), as well as jewelry, lingerie and accessories, which also can be custom-made. Material from the bride's dress, for example, can be used to make ring bearer's pillows.

At Allegra's you also can find the services of professional event planners. Becky Sue Moose of Classic Celebrations, for example, is one of several wedding consultants who can be available at the shop for a fee, to help coordinate your entire affair. Ettenson suggests that, weather permitting, this include a walk through town by the bridal party on the way to the reception, a very European custom. Distances are short, and the whole town participates, hailing and cheering the happy couple on their way. *Viva la mariage!*

Another kind of one-stop shopping experience is available at Hunt Country Celebrations, a group of 38 services providers who work mainly in the area between Warrenton and Middleburg, Virginia, but who are available to plan celebrations of all types and sizes anywhere in the Washington region.

The organization includes event planners, caterers, photographers, rental service companies, videographers, florists, bakers, gown and tuxedo stores, entertainment firms, makeup consultants and others. Its members can provide transportation ranging from horse-drawn carriages to limousines to yachts and can create your celebration in settings ranging from stately mansions to quaint country inns to a working horse ranch. Though it specializes in weddings, HCC will plan virtually any celebration, from family reunions and special birthdays and anniversaries to an occasion specially designed for you.

cleanup charges can also spell expensive overtime fees. Planners will oversee all vendor contracts and develop realistic timelines that will guard against additional costs.

3. PROTECTING YOUR INVESTMENT

If you hire an event planner, you will have someone on site to ensure that what you planned will be executed. Your affair is a celebration, not a job, so why take on the responsibility of checking that the flowers are placed exactly where you want them, that food is served on time, or the bartender isn't soliciting tips? After investing so much time and effort, not to mention money, in your event, you should be able to mingle with guests, eat in peace and dance the night away. You can't handle the details and enjoy yourself, too. Moreover, leave it to an experienced eye to anticipate potential problems and to respond effectively. Under most circumstances, a good planner can handle any curve without the guests, even the host, suspecting something was amiss.

4. PROVIDING DIFFERENT LEVELS OF SERVICE

Event planners, of course, can provide you with different levels of service. You can hire someone to design your celebration from start to finish, including coordination of all vendors and on-site execution. On the other hand, you can hire someone just to help you select a venue and decorate it. If you require assistance with mailing invitations and tracking responses, you can hire a planner to take over that segment of your event. You can also consult with a planner about how best to meet the needs of the disabled.

You should not, however, expect a messenger service. Event planners don't sign on to run errands or to tie bows on your party favors. If you require this type of assistance, they will be happy to oblige, but you probably will be charged accordingly.

A QUESTION OF FEES

PLANNER FEES. Most planners charge a flat fee for full or partial planning or on-site coordination. An hourly fee generally is charged for consultation only. As with other aspects of your celebration, your costs for a planner could range from hundreds to thousands of dollars, depending on your needs.

The best and most experienced planners are not cheap. If you are fairly knowledgeable and confident about what you want and the type of assistance you need, you can pursue someone less experienced. But if you are planning a large affair in which you will invest considerable time and money, you will be wise to hire a fully experienced planner to help you. This is not the time to choose someone breaking into the business or whose experience is limited to planning her own successful wedding.

VENDOR FEES. If you feel that the prices of vendors recommended by a planner are unreasonably high, tell the planner how you feel. A good event planner will be happy for your candor.

Some prospective clients worry that planners will try to steer them to expensive service providers because the planner receives rebates or discounts for doing so. That might be the case, although it is doubtful. Most planners pass savings on to their customers. If you have concerns, however, you should put them on the table at the outset.

As with any other volume purchase, the more you buy, the better the price. An event planner who uses specific vendors with regularity may get a better price than an individual planning his or her own event. But good planners do not jeopardize their hard-earned reputations because someone may pass on a discount to them. They make recommendations based on your budget and your needs and on the expertise of the vendor. They are there to make your life easier, not harder. ◆

CHAPTER V

Catering to Your Wishes

*A man hath no better thing under the sun, than to eat,
and to drink, and to be merry.*

— ECCLESIASTES

THROUGH THE AGES, breaking bread with family and friends is how special occasions have been celebrated the world over. So, too, with your party. The quality and quantity of the food you provide, as well as how it is presented and served, will be central to the merriment of your guests, to say nothing of the size of your bill. Clearly, paying close attention to catering questions will be one of your more important chores.

Consider, for example, the simple (and therefore easily overlooked) matter of double-checking the date, time and location of your event and ensuring that all is confirmed with the caterer as well as with other service providers. As with all things human, mistakes—and resulting disasters—can happen. I know of one couple who arrived at the swanky country club that they had rented for their wedding reception only to find no caterer there. He somehow had gotten the date wrong, and nobody had confirmed with him as the day drew near. In the end, the local pizza parlor came to the rescue, and a good time was had by all. But the gorgeous day the couple had planned was lost forever (though it is doubtful that any guest will ever forget their wedding). The moral: Assume nothing.

Washington is a party town, with caterers in heavy demand for personal, political, diplomatic, business and government receptions. The good news is that fine caterers abound, resulting in considerable choice and keen competition. The bad news is that some of the most popular catering companies can be booked a year or more in advance, so you would do well to begin your search as soon as you know the date of your celebration.

You may already have a list of potential caterers in mind because of impressions they've made at events you've attended or because of recommendations from family and friends. That can be exceedingly valuable information, but it can also be a mistake to think that your search largely ends there. For one thing, your experiences at others' celebrations do not include what went on behind the scenes, which may not always have been pretty. For another, recommendations of family and friends may not fit your budget or other preferences, and even some people close to you may be reluctant to discuss unpleasant experiences they may have had with their own parties.

So it's worth some additional effort to find the right caterer for your occasion. Needless to say, whichever company you choose should have a talented chef to provide beautifully prepared and presented food and a well-trained wait staff to serve it graciously and efficiently. Beyond this, however, caterers vary widely. Some excel at large, lavish affairs while others do better with smaller, intimate gatherings. Some are full-service firms, others partial-service companies. Some specialize in particular foods, whether for certain times of day or specific ethnic groups, while others concentrate on corporate events rather than personal celebrations. Each obviously has different strengths.

FULL-SERVICE FIRMS. Full-service caterers provide food, beverages, equipment, linens, glassware, china and cutlery as well as service staff. If you wish, they will also recommend all other service providers—florists, musicians, photographers and the like—within your price range, and they even can provide some event planning and limited help to orchestrate the actual event. Choosing a full-service caterer, therefore, works especially well for larger affairs, particularly if you prefer not to use an event or wedding coordinator.

For weddings, though, even some of the finest full-service caterers, such as Bill Homan of Design Cuisine, think it wiser to have someone other than the caterer manage the affair. "Hiring a wedding coordinator is the best investment you can make," Homan says. "They'll handle aspects of your wedding that you never even thought about . . . They take care of everything from the church and ceremony to the reception, to protocol issues and proper attire, and more, depending on your needs."

Full-service caterers are plentiful in Washington, but most short lists of top-of-the-line firms would include Design Cuisine, Federal City Caterers, Susan Gage, Occasions, Paris Caterers and Catering by Windows.

PARTIAL-SERVICE FIRMS. Partial-service caterers begin with those who simply prepare food to be dropped off at your home or other event site (or picked up by you, should you prefer that for, say, buffet brunches or smaller dinner parties). Such foods are provided not just by catering firms but also by an array of other outlets (some of which are also full-service caterers), from Dean & DeLuca and Giant Gourmet Someplace Special to Sutton Place Gourmet, Whole Foods or your favorite local delicatessen. Some partial-service caterers also provide other services—some staff to wait on guests and/or clean up afterward, china, glassware and cutlery or their disposable equivalents, or a chef to prepare or finish the food at your home or other site. Partial service means just that. You can find partial service firms that offer limited additional options, but in general they will not provide help with every aspect of your celebration.

SPECIALTY FIRMS. Specialty caterers generally are distinguished by the kinds of foods or groups they serve. For some examples:

◆ **PREFERRED MEALS.** Many people choose not to eat certain foods, and meatless meals are becoming more and more popular. Gail Naftalin, owner of Gail's Vegetarian Catering, prepares a hearty antipasto consisting of marinated vegetables. Such menu items certainly lower costs and are much appreciated by guests who restrict their diet to non-meat dishes.

◆ **LIGHTER MEALS.** Mr. Omelette mainly prepares omelettes for breakfasts and brunches, along with pancakes, French toast or Belgian waffles. Such menus are popular for bridal showers or even engagement parties, but the company also offers pasta and crepe menus for dinner. In addition, owners David and Jennifer Model recently added The Perfect Grind, a cappucino and smoothie bar service, to complement their menus. Cappucino and dessert parties are inexpensive (though the firm has minimum charges), easy to execute and great fun. Smoothies can make welcome additions to kids' celebrations, such as birthday parties or bar and bat mitzvahs. If budget is a dominant issue, having a breakfast, brunch or dessert party can solve your problem.

◆ **ETHNIC FOODS.** Serving the dishes of your heritage is a wonderful way to add to the festivities, and some also need to ensure that food is prepared according to religious ritual, as with kosher affairs.

Washingtonians have many choices for ethnic

celebrations, not least because of the expertise firms have developed serving the international community. Consider the popular Paris Caterers, owned by William deParis and his wife Rebecca, who hails from Puerto Rico and who has a special interest in international cuisine. Beyond traditional events for many others, Paris has prepared Indian, Turkish and Moroccan dishes and events for a variety of embassies and international groups. In Style Caterers also serves international fare and a "more eclectic menu than most caterers," says owner Denise Thorn, and fête accomplie catering does a good number of events at the Mexican Cultural Institute.

Roberto Torres of Better Events, on the other hand, has a unique approach to catering for the international community: His firm will do everything but the cooking. Some clients prefer dishes from restaurants dedicated to their homeland specialties, Torres says, so that's where he acquires the food. The restaurants—which generally are ill equipped to provide full catering services or, in most cases, adequate space for large parties—are pleased to accommodate, he adds. The restaurant prepares the food. Torres serves it and manages every other aspect of your event. Of course, your own favorite Latin, Italian, Jewish, Asian, Indian, Ethiopian, Lebanese or other ethnic restaurant is also a good place for you to look for a partial-service caterer, particularly for parties at your home.

For kosher affairs, some synagogues permit only approved caterers to prepare meals for events held at the temple; Adas Israel, the area's largest conservative synagogue, for example, requires using Carole Ash's The Artful Party, which works out of the synagogue kitchen. At other sites, however, a number of firms—such as Charles Levine Caterers and Sue Fischer of Catering by Windows—specialize in kosher affairs, and some venues have chefs who are experienced at kosher and other ethnic cooking. Melrose at the Park Hyatt, for example, pro-

vided wonderful kosher food for the wedding of a colleague's daughter at that hotel. For orthodox Jewish celebrations, there are caterers approved by the Rabbinical Council of Greater Washington. The organization provides a list of the companies under its supervision on its web site (*See Directory on p. 96*). That's how a friend's wife found a caterer for one of the seven days of celebrations—called *shevah brachot*, after the seven blessings recited during Jewish nuptials—that follow orthodox weddings.

◆ **BUSINESS GROUPS.** Another specialty company, Who's Cookin'? Catering, owned by Deetsie Chrapaty and Joe Malhotra, works only with corporate clients. It provides breakfasts, lunches, receptions and dinners, whether for 8 or 800. It also acts as consultant to companies that wish to purchase their own catering equipment or dinnerware and serving pieces or that want to install their own kitchens.

THE SHORT LIST

You should develop a short list of caterers in the category best suited to your event and then jot down specifics of your celebration—date, venue, estimated number of guests, budget range—as well as your likes and dislikes. The caterer will need to know all of this, just as you will need to know if he or she is licensed by local or state health authorities to prepare and/or serve food. You also should ask whether the caterer can sell or serve alcoholic beverages; in metropolitan Washington, each jurisdiction has its own regulations governing alcohol, and in some cases you may need to buy liquor yourself. In addition, you should ask about the caterer's insurance, what it covers and if you can be named as an additional insured. (*See Chapter XVI, Contracts and Insurance.*)

Once you have your short list, call and schedule meetings to discuss your event. For large affairs such as weddings, it is wise to meet with at least three firms (but not more than five—too many choices can be confusing). You may wish to draft a scorecard to grade those you interview, gauging the qualities that you value most, from reputation, cost and culinary expertise to human resources, creativity, communication and rapport with the person assigned to you. The simple grid could look like this:

	FIRM NO. 1	FIRM NO. 2	FIRM NO. 3
Reputation			
Cost			
Culinary Expertise			
Creativity			
Human Resources			
Rapport			
TOTAL			

You can use a numeric system, say from one to five, with five as the best mark. While the overall score will no doubt make your decision easier, you would do well to pay special attention to the "rapport" grade. It's of the utmost importance to feel entirely at ease with the caterer's representative, who should be experienced with events comparable to yours, fully understand your tastes or special requests, and be sensitive to any notable relationships with family or friends. If you're not compatible with this person, you could be courting disaster on this important and expensive aspect of your event.

REQUESTS FOR PROPOSALS

Once you have your final candidates, ask each firm to submit a proposal based on the event details you have provided. (Don't worry about telling caterers that you are bidding your event with competitors. It's a common practice that caterers are comfortable with.) Design Cuisine's Homan stresses the particu-

lar importance of being candid about budget. "You don't have to be specific, but you need to give us a range," he says, adding: "Please, don't say you don't have a budget. Caterers can't work that way."

Review each bid carefully—comparing apples to apples. At first blush, one firm's proposal may appear less expensive, but it may not include charges that are part of another firm's bid. Make sure, for instance, to note the size, hourly charge and time allotted by each firm for the wait staff, which is generally billed in 4-hour increments, and don't forget to check overtime rates. Sometimes a lower bid will reflect reduced staff, which can make a notable difference in service at your affair. On the other hand, if you don't desire the level of service proposed, a good way to cut costs is to trim staff. Beware, however, of cutting staff solely because you plan to have a buffet. A buffet does not necessarily mean you'll need less help. Staff will still be needed to pour water and wine, to refill the buffet, sometimes to offer seconds to those already seated or to serve dessert and to bus tables and clean up afterwards. Buffets, in fact, sometimes can be more expensive than seated meals, because you can't control portion size. If some guests serve themselves too generously, you will have to keep adding food until everyone is fed.

You similarly should note rental charges and what they include. Some people tend to view these as routine items—until they get the bill. I have a friend, for example, who ended up paying a not-so-routine sum for silk tablecloths and napkins that were never specifically discussed by the caterer or wedding planner. Similarly, make sure that rented items are of comparable value. Will you get those silk tablecloths and napkins with one caterer and twill with another? Are the quality and design of the tableware similar? Will each caterer be providing decorative items for buffet tables? Unless you don't care about the size of your final bill, be sure such questions are addressed.

THE MENU AND DÉCOR

After you pick the successful candidate, your initial meeting with the caterer should focus on the menu, probably the most costly item in your budget, which you presumably will already have discussed in a general way during the proposal process. Just as there is more to selecting a caterer than planning a menu, there is more to planning a menu than your budget or the type of celebration. For example:

◆ Your venue will influence what food is served, and how. If you plan a party at home and space there is tight, that may limit you to passing hors d'oeuvres. A larger home will permit a variety of foods on a buffet, while spacious gardens or rented halls will allow for tables and chairs for either a buffet or a seated meal.

◆ Some strikingly presented foods may work wonderfully in restaurants but not for 200 relatives and friends, so if you are planning a sizable affair, be careful to choose dishes that can be prepared well in quantity.

◆ Serving food of which your-cousin-the-cardiologist would approve is increasingly the trend. It is not always easy to satisfy all of your guests' preferences in this regard, but you should do as much as possible. You certainly should, for one example, include a vegetarian dish or dishes for those whom you know do not eat meat or fish or who have certain food allergies.

◆ Another way to approach this question is to offer a choice of entrées at a seated dinner, which is also becoming popular. If you do so, however, it will add to the cost.

◆ As a rule, avoid foods that are too heavy, especially at large celebrations such as weddings, since that will not help make for the liveliest of guests.

◆ For the same reason—and not just to save costs—serve satisfying but not excessively large portions.

◆ A nice touch is to prepare one course or buffet dish from a family recipe, made all the better by the presence and acknowledgment of the particular loved one.

◆ An outdoor event in August is no time to offer salads made with mayonnaise or other foods that spoil easily in warm weather.

Otherwise, there is virtually no limit within your budget to the variety of food that can be served at your celebration. The choice is yours—traditional, ethnic or trendy. Follow your instincts, and don't be afraid to exercise a little flare. Good caterers will help with recommendations on all these matters and much more, such as holding out as long as possible on final menu choices until you have checked for the newest food items, recipes and presentation methods. Unless you firmly oppose something, the caterer's counsel usually will serve you well. They will advise you on the best use of the space at your home or elsewhere, on wine or other beverages, on dishes with which their customers have had the best luck, and on how talks or toasts or entertainment might best be scheduled. But don't count on a caterer for more than advice about the schedule. More often than not, you will need someone experienced in special events, a wedding coordinator or a trusted friend to orchestrate the actual details of your celebration.

The same holds for choosing linens, tableware and table decorations. Caterers not only will show you samples of materials and other items and advise you on how best to use what, but they sometimes will issue special pleas, as one caterer does, for example, on the matter of color matching for weddings. "*Please* tell your readers that it's not necessary to match your bridesmaid's *anything to anything*," stresses this professional, who has given this advice more than once.

While matching dresses and tablecloths may not be important, having the flowers work well with the rest of the table décor certainly will be. So you should make sure that the florist, as well as the caterer, meets you at the venue for the event when you begin making such decisions. Mind you, you probably will be wiser not to make final décor decisions until about three months before the celebration itself; something new is always coming out, and it is good not to lock yourself in too early.

TASTINGS AND WALKTHROUGHS

Once you have made decisions on menus and décor, however, it is wise to get out of the way and let the catering firm do its job. As Deborah Allen of Federal City Caterers puts it: "Be secure in your own taste, but once you have done the planning, you have to relinquish control. You need to trust your caterer."

That's not easy for everyone. Some people, who simply cannot see the event in their heads, are tempted to keep looking over the caterer's shoulder every inch of the way. As Design Cuisine's Homan says, "It's very hard for some people to visualize how things will look. That's why I like to show people what they'll be getting."

You should be reassured by the fact that, even after you make firm decisions, you will still have two chances to see what you actually will be getting, especially for large celebrations like weddings. One chance will come with the tasting, usually held about a month before an event. Tastings are expensive, and some companies understandably are reluctant to do them for smaller-group events. But if your affair is a large one that will put a hefty dent in your bank account, the caterer certainly should provide this service, just as the florist should have your floral arrangement there for the occasion. The best caterers will set up the food and tables exactly as they will be on the day of your party. If you are having seated tables of 10 but only three people are attending the tasting, you will be at a table set for 10, with food, linens,

tableware, flowers, other decorations and serving trays as they will be at the event itself. There should be no surprises.

The other step that should make you more comfortable about the event will be the final vendor meeting and walkthrough at the celebration site, usually done 10 days or so before the affair. As many vendors as possible should attend this meeting—caterer, florist, event planner, rental firm, even musicians. It's essential to have no misunderstandings, for example, about where musicians will set up, especially if the caterer had been planning to have something else in the space the musicians think best for them. The last thing you want at the actual event is conflict over a question like that. The walkthrough should clear up all such matters and ensure that everyone knows what is expected of them.

In the end, if you are like most people, budget will force you to make some decisions that you would have liked to avoid, whether about food or beverages or staffing or whatever. The best of anything is expensive, and whether it is worth the price or not is irrelevant if the price is beyond your reach. But always keep one thing in mind: Good taste is not expensive. It takes as much work to produce an event on a tight budget as it does to produce one when money is no object. I recently heard about a woman who was convinced that her budget would rule out a particular caterer, one she had always wanted to do her daughter's wedding. To her surprise, the caterer accepted the challenge of producing a beautiful wedding on a tight budget. The woman was delighted.

"Was it pretty?" the caterer says. "Yes. Was it expensive? No. In fact the total cost came in a little under budget. Good taste goes a long way."

That's the kind of caterer everyone needs. ◆

CHAPTER VI

Picking Flowers
(And Alternatives)

Flowers are lovely; love is flower-like

—SAMUEL TAYLOR COLERIDGE

FLOWERS NOURISH THE senses and the soul. That's why they are the stuff of poetry and why fragrant blossoms and delicate petals can heighten the glory and enhance the memories of celebrations. So how can you ensure that flowers add such beauty to your special occasion?

Some may think that the answer is strictly a matter of money. There's no question that flowers themselves can be expensive, especially for large affairs, and the services of a talented florist do not come cheap. In general, most people don't understand how labor intensive floral design is, and they don't understand costs. But there are numerous ways to economize without sacrificing loveliness. You can use seasonal flowers grown locally, eliminating large airfreight bills. For containers, you can employ antiques or other treasured pieces of your own or borrowed from family or friends, rather than paying often significant rental fees. The truly adventurous or the financially strapped can even pick their own seasonal flowers (or have good friends do it for them), especially for more intimate affairs, and cost-cutting techniques by no means end there.

You should keep in mind, though, that there is no replacement for a talented professional florist, who should be able to offer creative solutions to budget issues as well as alternatives to flowers, which in some cases may be necessary. While you may long for bushels of blooms in a room, on tables or at a ceremony site, if you know that guests—or, worse, you—are allergic to certain fragrance or pollens, you may have to choose other ways to add drama to your event. Allergic guests, moreover, will appreciate it if the florist removes stamens—the pollen-producing parts of flowers—from all blooms.

If money is no object, there are some famous florists who not only will produce gorgeous floral arrangements but also will design your entire celebration. Robert Isabell and David Tutera of New York and Stanlee Gatti of San Francisco represent the utmost in stylish event planning. They produce events for royalty and the rest of the world's rich and famous. They also command staggering fees, for which they will create a unique event especially for you, comparable to no other.

WASHINGTON'S OWN

Fortunately, Washington has its share of talented florists who also produce events. Multiflor, located in Virginia but serving the metropolitan area and beyond, for example, is a medium-sized floral décor company that can do an intimate dinner for two or a 300-person wedding at the Ritz Carlton in Montego Bay, Jamaica. Run by Nick Perez, the company is able to address everything from linens to lighting to draping a room with fabric. Jessie

Bailey of JLB Florist, also based in Virginia, has worked on Inaugural events and some of the most chi-chi parties in the Washington area. In addition to floral design, Bailey is especially adept at non-floral, architectural and sculptural orchestration and at acting as liaison between a client and all event vendors to pull together the entire look of a celebration.

Some clients are inclined to work with a florist/event designer; others, particularly when it comes to weddings, prefer to work with a wedding consultant and a florist. Whichever you prefer, remember that each florist will have his or her own style and will excel with specific looks. If you are a minimalist, beware of the florist who produces fabulous Victorian designs and Mussie Tussies (holders for a small bouquet, usually made for the mother of a bride). Caít Oliver, Creative Director of Encore Décor, believes you should think of a florist as you would an artist. "Floral design is a very visual process. We try to help our clients understand all the elements that will make a specific look come together," she says. Colors and textures are important, but Oliver says, "It's important to use what's appropriate for the space or venue being used. Sometimes less is more."

"Most clients start off by telling you they want their event to be different" and little else, says Nick Perez of Multiflor, adding: "The most difficult client is an ambiguous one. The details of any celebration make the difference." In other words, you can't expect to achieve a distinctive floral décor if you haven't decided how much of your budget will be allocated for flowers or alternative decorations and what you especially like and dislike, what defines you. So it's important to spend some time first researching and thinking about your preferences and budget.

Many publications and web sites can be consulted. Scour them for good design ideas and prices before you meet with a florist—and try to be realistic. Oversized arrangements don't work in small spaces.

Flowers should complement, not dominate. Their fragrance, too, should not overwhelm, so be careful about selecting blooms with strong scents, particularly for food tables.

THE PERFECT MATCH

It's important to begin searching for a florist at least six to eight months before a wedding—and longer if the florist will also be the primary planner. Less time is needed for other occasions (this will depend, of course, on the magnitude of the celebration), but a month is the minimum for a simple celebration. That will give you the best chance of securing your selection of flowers and other greenery, as well as the florist of your choice. That's not to say that some florists can't turn on a dime. Jesse Bailey says, "Being asked to produce flowers for a high-profile event in less than a few days is what keeps this business fun and interesting and helps keep us on our toes." But that's the exception, not the rule.

To start, get recommendations from friends and family. Caterers usually can also recommend several vendors who excel within your style and budget, as can hotel catering personnel. Some sites, such as Washington's Mayflower Hotel, have their own florists. Courtney Zellmer, who took over at the Mayflower from her mentor, Jackie Kelleher, does outstanding work for all types of celebrations, from weddings to corporate events to many kinds of social occasions. She also will travel to other states to help with your floral needs. Once you have developed your short list, plan to interview two or three of your top prospects, and make sure to meet at the florist's place of business. That way you not only can look at pictures and portfolios but also see current projects and the quality of stock used. The variety and freshness of the flowers should be first rate.

A good florist will ask lots of questions about venues, table linens, lighting and other elements. He or she should venture forth to see the particulars firsthand. If the work is for a wedding, the florist will likely ask about the design and fabric of the bride's dress and take her complexion, hairdo and makeup into consideration. What the bridal party is wearing and the attire of the wedding couple's parents may also be weighed. After a review of all the details, a recommendation within your budget will follow. Be sure it's specific and in writing. Every detail should be itemized—choice of flowers, colors and prices. You may also want to include mention of any substitutions to be used in the event your original choice of flowers is not available at the last minute. Even though such itemization can be a painstaking process, you'll be pleased in the long run.

MAKING BUDGET

Good florists also will help you take an economical approach if that is necessary or desired. They will know which flowers are in season and grow in the area. While air transportation has enabled the availability of global, seasonal fresh flowers, shipment can add dramatically to costs. The containers in which flowers are arranged can also enlarge your bill significantly, so you might want to use your own. Silver teapots, antique vases, childhood pottery and other containers can all make meaningful as well as beautiful receptacles for your floral arrangements. Just be sure to have someone watch over them after the event, or a guest could walk off with a family heirloom. Should you decide to rent, however, Jesse Bailey of JLB Florist has what I consider the best collection of containers to enhance the beauty of your floral décor.

As with all aspects of a celebration, economy can be achieved through creativity. Economical centerpieces for occasional seating and pub tables can be made by grouping a few stems cut fairly short and tied with a pretty ribbon. Lay the tiny bouquets directly on the tables, surround them with a few votive candles and you've got a great look for a pittance. Bigger is not necessarily better.

If you're planning a wedding, you may want to inquire if you can share floral and candle expenses with another couple. Many ceremony venues hold more than one wedding a day. So long as you can agree on style, sharing costs (of all but personal flowers) can make a significant difference to your bank account. You might also consider using some flowers twice. For instance, ceremony site arrangements can be used at a reception to decorate food tables or to enhance some other area.

Flowering potted plants and greenery are another cost-cutting alternative to fresh-cut flowers. Savvy hostesses make the most of this option. A plant—or several, depending on size—wrapped in a stylish piece of fabric or a matching table napkin tied with a pretty ribbon, string or yarn can make a lovely centerpiece. Greenery such as large ferns, or birds of paradise leaves, bamboo or palm fronds standing tall in a slender clear vessel on a buffet table is striking and easy on the budget. (As an added bonus, bamboo has been said to represent good fortune, a perfect element for any celebration, and it also works especially well, as do certain grasses and large leaf plants, with Asian-inspired menus.)

If you've got nerves of steel, especially in the event of a wedding, and an equivalent dose of creativity, you can pick your own flowers. For this, you need to use the available blooms of the picking season (usually July, August and September) and have the time and ability to design your own arrangements (or the talent of a very good friend or group of friends). But call before you head for an area flower garden like Butler's Orchard, Farmhouse Flowers or Frank's Produce. Farmhouse owner Dave Dowling recommends calling as soon as possible. An appointment is required, and there is a minimum charge.

Those choosing this route must be a hearty bunch. Arranging your own flowers demands considerable creativity or a genuine ability to accept whatever you get. How would you react, for instance, if the gorgeous roses you envisioned have closed heads (or "bullheads" that will never open) and are not available in the color you wanted? Similarly, are you (or your friends) willing to de-thorn the roses, no small chore? As my sister Andrea Graham reminded me, "Roses are beautiful and my favorite, but the thorns can bring tears to your eyes if you touch them and can totally destroy a beautiful dress." Or what if someone has beaten you to the glorious blooms you've been dreaming about. Clearly, you need to call ahead about what is available, and in what quantities and colors, as well as about any equipment required for picking. Dowling says that while Farmhouse is a cut-flower farm, "it is not a home and garden showplace." If you can simply approach the question with a *ces't la vie* attitude, this is an extremely inexpensive choice compared with using a retail florist. It works best when a relatively modest number of stems are required for your celebration.

IN ADDITION TO FRESH FLOWERS

Other elements are sometimes used to complement fresh flowers. For example:

PLANTS AND TREES. Large plants and trees are often used as an additional decorative element or to transform space. Ficus, palm and olive trees, for instance, are used successfully to create an entryway, decrease the size of a room, hide equipment or spruce up drab or ugly corners and walls. Green and flowering plants are pretty and can be used in all sorts of ways to enhance a room.

ICE SCULPTURES. The aesthetic value of ice sculptures is often in the eye of the beholder, but they nonetheless are widely used, mostly as large centerpieces. You can find them on buffet tables, in reception areas or as baskets and bowls to hold fruit, chocolate and such.

The sculptures come in all shapes and sizes and can be customized to include the names or initials of honorees. They can also be made to complement a theme or to incorporate flowers and greenery, and they can even be attractively illuminated. How effective they are will depend on the talent of the designer and the clarity of the ice used.

Since the average celebration lasts about five hours, there's no need to be concerned about a sculpture's longevity. Although it will depend on the design and density of the piece, you generally can count on sculptures lasting six to eight hours. Of course, temperatures and other weather conditions will affect those destined for outdoor use.

ALTERNATIVES TO FRESH FLOWERS

If you can't use flowers because of allergies or choose not to use fresh blooms or greenery for other reasons, the options are limited only by your imagination, though not all are less expensive or as elegant as fresh blooms.

CANDLES. Candles, for instance, can be striking, but they are not cheap, especially for the long-burning and dripless variety. You can, for example, spend a substantial amount on pillar candles, particularly since you'll probably need three or more per table and will require something to put them in or on. In the end, the expense will probably equal the average centerpiece cost.

PHOTOGRAPHS. Copies of old photos in antique frames—shots of a bride and groom as children growing up, of a 25th anniversary couple in their youths, of the streets where you lived for a neighborhood reunion—can provide wonderful touches and work either in centerpieces or on reception tables. Use little placards to explain the pictures to guests. Photos also add valuable dimensions to family reunions, memorial services and other occasions. *(See Chapter VIII.)*

CAKES. One school of thought holds that elegant or fun cakes work as wonderful centerpieces for each table, saving you money and doubling as dessert. Some bakers disagree about the savings on the cakes themselves, noting that the cost to decorate each one can more than make up for the expense of flowers or other decorations. Properly executed, individual cakes do make for a great look, especially at a seated wedding dinner, but your bill will depend on the intricacy of the decorations and on whether the cakes are purchased from a large commercial house or more expensive specialty baker *(See Chapter XI)*.

FRUIT. Fruit is another great substitute, and fresh fruit, which can be fashioned into attractive centerpieces, also can double as dessert. For seasonal touches, an arrangement of small pumpkins can be lovely and inexpensive in fall (and a non-fruit grouping of seashells in sand can conjure up thoughts of the seaside in spring or summer). Similarly, lemons and limes mixed with oranges, mounded in a water-filled clear bowl or vase, perhaps crowned by a floating candle, can make a striking centerpiece. These and other choices can satisfy both your budget and your aesthetic inclinations.

BALLOONS. Balloons are popular. They add color and are festive, but they, too, can sometimes be costly. They are best used for decoration in large spaces and to camouflage such things as an unattractive ceiling. Balloon designers can create arrangements to look like clouds, adorn entryways, or provide a burst of color in a drab corner. Balloons also can make a setting feel smaller if a room is too big for your event (few things are worse than a party in a space that's too large for the event and for the number of guests attending). Centerpieces made from balloons work best for theme parties, and they are a big hit with the corporate and younger sets. Some think they are somewhat out of their element for wedding table decorations and other more formal gatherings. As a rule, though, balloons are fun and add to the merriment.

SILK AND DRIED FLOWERS. Silk and dried flowers are yet another option, especially if you or your guests are allergic to fresh flowers. Unfortunately, silk flowers still suffer from the ugly-stepsister syndrome. While designers can produce lovely arrangements that look quite real, especially ones from J. Brown & Company, silk flowers often are considered taboo, particularly if scent is added to a bouquet. If you are thinking about using silk flowers to preserve, say, a bridal bouquet, there are firms in the area that do just that with fresh flowers. Dried floral arrangements can be pretty and effective, especially if you want a Victorian look, but unless you do the work to create them, this choice may not be a money-saving option.

For at-home entertaining, you can use all kinds of crystal, silver and collectible items to decorate food tables and reception areas. Doing so can reduce costs and produce special looks, particularly ones that complement holiday celebrations, while assuring comfort for even the most allergic guest.

A dear friend of mine, the late Terry Noack, who was a talented interior decorator and event producer, insisted that every celebration needs an element of surprise. "Whatever it is," he said, "there should be one drop-dead gorgeous piece for guests to see." Whether you choose fresh flowers, complementary plants, trees or ice sculptures or alternatives to fresh flowers, it's worth keeping that in mind. ◆

CHAPTER VII

Musical Effects

Music hath charms to sooth a savage breast,
To soften rocks, or bend a knotted oak

—WILLIAM CONGREVE

MUSIC ACTUALLY DOES more than sooth, soften or bend people or things. It makes hearts sing, feet move, fingers tap and spirits soar. It triggers memories, evokes eras and defines cultures. It is sheer fun—and it often can make or break your celebration.

The trick is to select the music that fits your event and venue. Thus a 12-piece band might be wonderful for a large wedding, bat mitzvah or reunion but would overwhelm a Sweet 16 party. A large band would, moreover, present serious problems if the venue space were modest, since guests might not be able to hear their own voices. Conversely, a solo harpist or a flute and violin might provide the perfect touch for a pre-dinner reception but prove terribly inadequate for a large affair. At the wrong time and place, in other words, delightful music can be a flop, so you must always consider music in context.

You also should hear the musicians (or the deejay, if that is your preference) in person—and, if possible, in a setting similar to the one you plan to use— before making any decisions. Videotapes of bands provided by booking agencies can be quite useful as screening devices, but they are far from sufficient for final selections. A magnificent band on tape, for example, may sound quite different in person and may have switched vocalists or made other changes. Similarly, a band that is exciting on tape might be too loud in person, especially in a room with the wrong acoustics. Because of acoustical questions, in fact, you would be wise to listen to the music at one or more celebrations at the venue you have chosen. It will give you a better sense of the type of music and instruments that do—or do not—work well there. If you are renting a public space, such as a historic mansion or gardens, moreover, you should ask if there are any instrument, noise or dancing restrictions.

All celebration music, of course, is not intended for dancing. Weddings, for example, begin with music for the most important part of the event, the marriage ceremony—the prelude while guests are seated, the processional for the wedding party, music during the ceremony, and the recessional and postlude. If you are planning a religious ceremony, be sure to check with the house of worship about what is appropriate and permitted as you ponder whether to have a solo singer, an instrumentalist, a small group or some combination. A number of musicians in the Washington area specialize in ceremony music, whether for traditional affairs or unique ones such as Celtic weddings, and they are a good source of help. The Riverside Brass, which has offices in Washington and Virginia, for example, has prepared a guide to ceremony music. It contains information on such matters as musical options, when and for how long to play each, instrument choices, whether to have a soloist and whether to invite a friend or family member to perform.

There are also musicians who play for children's birthday parties, for home entertaining (when you want to do something more than play personal CDs or tapes), for corporate get-togethers and other non-dancing parties. The largest hunt you will engage in for the right music, however, is likely to involve a big bash and dancing by family and friends. For this you would do well to keep several things in mind:

◆ **BRIDGING DECADES.** Make sure that the musicians or the DJ are adept at mixing music across decades, so that 70-year-old aunts and 13-year old cousins and everybody in between feels like they are part of the celebration.

◆ **GROUP DANCES.** For similar reasons, it's always a joy when guests get involved in group dances, whether ethnic favorites like Italian tarantellas, Jewish horas or Greek Zorba dances or home-grown fun like the electric slide, line dances or Cajun Zydeco. Indeed, a scholarly case has been made that people who move together to the same beat tend to bond, which is precisely what you want to happen. Even if guests require lessons for a group dance, those could be provided during a band break, so long as a band member or someone else is adept at doing the teaching.

◆ **THE LEADER OF THE BAND.** In the case of weddings or bar and bat mitzvahs, using a bandleader as the master of ceremonies is quite popular. He or she handles all the warm and fuzzy stuff—introducing the newlyweds, the parents, the first dance, the dances with parents and the cake cutting, as well as those giving toasts or roasts or lighting candles. (You and/or your party planner will, of course, have to provide an event timeline, with names and pronunciations of those honored.) It's a key job, one that is certainly as important as the quality of the band's musical performance—but not one for which an agency's videotape is of value. Checking an emcee's reper-

toire and demeanor is thus another important reason why you should observe prospective musicians in person.

I confess that I am not a fan of using taped music, except under the direction of a DJ and when entertaining teenagers or a small group at home. Though Washingtonians are a fairly affluent bunch, few, if any, can afford *NSYNC any other way. In that case, playing selections from your personal musical collection is fine and, in fact, says something to guests about you and your interests.

In most other cases, however, I would encourage you to scrimp on something else if you have to in order to have live music, even if only for a short period. There's no substitute for it. For instance, you can play music for dancing only during a reception and then adjourn for dinner. Guests will be energized from the music and dancing—a great segue for lively dinner table conversation. Another cost-saving possibility: Consider using one musician who plays an instrument but is accompanied by computer-generated sounds. This option, staged properly, can be extremely effective.

FINDING THE RIGHT PEOPLE

There are many ways to find the right music for you. Sometimes you'll discover the perfect band at someone else's celebration or through recommendations from family, friends, a party planner, catering director or other service provider. You also can get much information on musicians, including those videos, from entertainment agencies, or you can turn to bridal shows, web sites and magazines. In the end, though, the most important factor will be the judgment you make in person, whether while visiting other affairs, going to local clubs or during an audition. To be sure that you don't miss a beat (pun intended), you should consider the following during your musical search:

◆ **THE VALUE OF AN AGENCY.** Booking musicians directly can be less expensive than using an agent—but at what price? Will the musicians you auditioned be the same ones who show up for your celebration? What happens if the vocalist or leader takes sick, runs off to Brazil or joins the Air Force Band? In some instances, unfortunately, musical groups disband, leaving you high and dry. Your deposit—usually required at the time of booking, sometimes a year in advance—also could be in jeopardy. If you know the musicians personally, of course, booking directly can work well. But in other cases, using an agent provides you with an advocate and assures you of the best result should problems arise. There are various reliable, longtime agencies in the Washington area, including Glen Pearson Productions & Floating Opera, Bialek's Music, the Siebel Group and the Washington Talent Agency.

◆ **THE EGO QUESTION.** Is the group comfortable providing background music only? Some groups, particularly those with vocalists, expect audiences to observe them, not talk to fellow guests. That attitude can present problems for many celebrations. So be sure to tell the group leader exactly what the occasion is and the role you envision for the music—and remember to discuss volume levels as well. Few things can hurt an affair as much as having to shout to have a conversation.

◆ **WHAT HAPPENS DURING BREAKS?** While many discuss which songs they want played, whether the group will take requests, the number of sets during the contracted-for period and the length of each set and each break, less thought generally is given to what happens during those breaks. What will be played? Tacky taped music can rear its ugly head here. If you can tolerate that, so be it. If not, you might consider investing additional funds for, say, a roving guitarist or violinist or for music of your heritage, whether klezmer melodies, bagpipes, a steel pan or African drums. It can keep the momentum going and add a wonderful touch to your celebration.

◆ **OTHER BAND ISSUES.** What you find agreeable on a number of other fronts should also come into play. What will the group be wearing? Will any signage be displayed on music stands? Will any background banners be used? Offering cards to those who request them is fine, but do you really want the group advertising during your affair? Similarly, will any special effects be used? How do you feel about tiny bubbles, soap suds or fog wafting around? Would such elements be appropriate, safe, tasteful and, above all, acceptable to you?

◆ **DEEJAY CONCERNS.** Deejays are often used in place of live music when a younger audience is involved. The process for selecting one is similar to that for seeking an orchestra or band, though with some additional concerns involved. Is his or her equipment, for example, in good working order? If something goes wrong with it, the silence won't be golden. Does the equipment and sound booth or workspace look shabby? Will it fit in with your décor? Advertising or tacky signs could be more of a problem here, so be sure to discuss this thoroughly. If you are working through an agency, is the deejay an experienced spinner or a rookie? Prices should reflect the level of experience. Does the deejay use props? If so, what kind? Some may not be acceptable. What about his or her inventory? Is the collection varied, with nostalgic, classic and ethnic songs as well as current hits? Will he or she get guests involved?

As with other services, prices for music vary by season, by day of the week and by time of day as well as by the number of performers hired—obviously, 10-piece bands generally cost more than jazz quartets—and by how much they are in demand. As a rule, deejays are less expensive than live performers, but don't be fooled: A really good one can cost more than one or two live musicians. Whatever your choice, however, it is important to contract for your music as early as possible, since the most sought after musicians and deejays often are booked as much as a year in advance. ◆

CHAPTER VIII

Capturing the Memories

All photographs are there to remind us of what we forget.
— JOHN BERGER

A SPECIAL CELEBRATION can bring joy not simply during the event itself but for the rest of your life. The lifetime of pleasure comes, of course, from the memories captured by photography and videography, which means that your decisions on these matters will be of lasting importance. It is puzzling, then, why some people limit photography considerations to such events as weddings or bar mitzvahs, as if recording other life passages were unimportant, and why they too often fail to use old snapshots to enrich table decorations, invitations or other aspects of today's celebrations. *(See box on p. 52.)*

Because photos and footage matter so much—and because you don't get second chances to capture the occasions—you need to be careful in picking photographers, in ensuring that they have backup equipment, and in choosing the kind of photography appropriate to your event and your preferences. Hopefully, nobody still thinks photography is merely a matter of ordering this many 8x10s and that many wallet-size copies of formal poses. There are, after all, three kinds of cameras (still, digital and video) and two shooting styles (portraits and candid shots), which can result in three types of photographic records: formal poses and scenes of the day, photojournalism, or a pure storybook, or documentary account.

If you want a formal album of portraits and traditional celebration activities, you probably want a photographer with a still or digital camera for posed pictures and for shooting ceremonies and celebration rituals. Those who prefer a more spontaneous record of public and private moments at a wedding or reunion or milestone birthday should turn to photojournalism. Videography usually follows a storybook format and can also employ sound, adding another dimension to the memories. A combination of the approaches is used at many formal events and can, in fact, be employed at any celebration. In making your choices, however, you should consider the personality of the photographer as well as his or her technical prowess. For example:

THE PHOTO DIPLOMAT. Portraiture, which generally is used for weddings, bar and bat mitvahs and other formal affairs, is time-consuming, with two hours or more of shooting not uncommon. This requires a patient, diplomatic photographer, one who is comfortable with people, who can make subjects feel at ease and willing to follow direction. Don't forget that how a photographer treats guests can have an important effect on your event.

THE INVISIBLE BEING. Photojournalism, which can capture every touching moment—a falling tear, unabashed joy or a child's wonderment—is a very different matter. Still photographers who keep setting off flashes—and videographers with bright lights that generate heat—can be intrusive. You don't need diplomats for this but photographers who know how to become as invisible as possible. For still photographers, the problem is eased with telephoto lenses, allowing some shots to be taken at a distance, though how many is limited by lighting. With any photographer you are considering hiring, however, you should discuss limits on intrusiveness, which also will affect your affair.

A number of other factors need to be considered beyond the photographer's expertise. Indeed, there are enough good photographers in the Washington area to fill a stadium, so you should have little trouble choosing someone who is talented, compatible and in your price range. There are, of course, some highly creative, highly sought—and highly priced— photographers (sometimes charging tens of thousands of dollars) and others who do impressive work for above-average fees. If your heart is set on a particular photographer who is out of your price range, don't be shy about asking how to reduce costs; the tradeoffs may be worth it. Remember, however, that there are many good photographers here. You can get leads on them from friends, family, colleagues, web sites, magazines or bridal shows.[1]

Finding the right person may turn out to be easier than chores like scheduling photo sessions, corralling subjects or deciding where to shoot.

PORTRAITURE CHALLENGES

1. WHEN AND HOW MANY? Take the hours-long portrait sessions for formal affairs, especially weddings. They create several challenges. For example, you obviously don't want to miss a big part of your own special day or keep guests waiting too long to see you or to have their own pictures taken. You can handle this in several ways:

---

[1] *Even if you're not planning a wedding, bridal shows let you judge, in one place, a number of photographers' and videographers' bedside manners and portfolios, so some can be instantly eliminated while others go on your candidate list.*

◆ **BEFOREHAND.** The most common solution is to take formal pictures before the ceremony begins. While some still consider it bad luck for the groom to see the bride before the ceremony, spending a sizable part of your affair in a photo session isn't so great, either. (If you plan to have a reception and then a sit-down dinner, additional photos can, of course, be taken during the reception.) You can even take some formal pictures before the day of the event altogether, and if you are really superstitious, the bride and groom can be scheduled separately.

◆ **FEWER FORMAL SHOTS.** Limit your list of formal shots—of bride and groom, of bar or bat mitzvah boy or girl, of immediate family—but make sure that other photos are taken of additional family members and friends during the celebration. In that case, be sure to provide the photographer and/or videographer with a list of all persons to be photographed or interviewed and where they will be seated. This option may require some tough decisions, but it could save you lots of time and money.

◆ **AFTERWARD.** You also can take your formal photos after the wedding. Indeed, you can turn this into a romantic interlude, perhaps on your one-month anniversary. Arrange a late afternoon appointment at your photographer's studio. Follow the session with a candlelight dinner, and spend the night at a hotel (if possible, where you spent your wedding night). It's a great opportunity to celebrate all over again.

2. CORRALLING FAMILY AND FRIENDS. Whatever the celebration, corralling family and friends to pose for formal pictures can be difficult at best.

For large affairs, you need to develop—well ahead of time—a list of those to be included in such photos. In part, this is to make sure that nobody is offended; having to deal with angry family members or friends who are inadvertently left out can spoil the day. It is also designed, however, to make sure that photos are carefully scheduled. If you are shooting before a ceremony, subjects need to be told the schedule, so that they are ready and rounded up at the right time (a chore for the photographer's assistant or for someone in your party who might be willing to do it). You don't want to keep people waiting while others are being photographed; a timeline, with slots for each subject, is well worth the effort. Neglecting to schedule carefully could result in overtime for the photographer or videographer or, worse, insufficient time for all the shots you have planned.

It also can cause problems at less formal affairs. Remember that once the party starts, it's hard to get those you want photographed to focus on anything but having a good time. For my husband's retirement party, for example, two of our sons decided that, as a gift, they would hire a photographer to document the occasion. It was a wonderful present. The problem was that I had worn myself to a frazzle—and had failed to focus ahead of time on the photography. During the event, I found it almost impossible to get our family together for the one picture we wanted, and it was even harder to round up all the guests for a group shot. Fortunately, the photographer was up to the task and managed to get everyone to do as he asked. The resulting family picture is my all-time favorite, and the group shot of all who came is one that we treasure.

Using Existing Prints and Footage

Whether and how you might use existing prints and footage will depend on your event, but it's a popular practice that can add meaning and humor to a celebration and is guaranteed to be a crowd-pleaser.

A friend of mine, for example, attended a neighborhood reunion for 250—the "kids" (and their spouses) with whom he grew up in the 1940s and 1950s in Brooklyn, New York. The catering hall's walls were adorned with 2-foot and 3-foot matted blowups of old neighborhood landmarks, from the park where everyone played in their childhoods to the stores and hangouts on the main drag. All the flowers and fancy decorations in the world couldn't have matched those photos.

To celebrate milestone birthdays, baby pictures make great cake toppers; they can be fun, too, on invitations for a career promotion or retirement.

For your own wedding album or video, including parents' marriage pictures and snapshots from your childhoods can add drama and meaning as well. This would give you a combination of color and black-and-white photos or footage, which can be quite dramatic. Make sure, however, to discuss this possibility well ahead of time with the photographer or videographer and to pick old photos carefully.

A framed collage of family photos makes a great gift for a special wedding anniversary. In fact, photo collages make great gifts for many celebrations. The memories they evoke are priceless.

Spend some time on how you might use existing photography. You won't regret it.

3. LOCATION, LOCATION, LOCATION. Depending on where your event is held, your photographer or videographer will recommend desirable locations, with appropriate backgrounds, where formal pictures can be taken. Before agreeing, however, be sure to check out the locations yourself well before the day of the event. Hotels and other venues usually have several choices, but many are in public areas. You don't want the venue's normal conduct of business to infringe on your photo session.

You will also need to be sensitive to lighting questions, which can be particularly challenging when shooting outdoors. Indoor lighting is just as important but easier to control. Be sure to discuss all lighting in detail and how certain outside locations may be affected by insufficient or bright natural light. Sunsets, for example, make dynamic backdrops but can play havoc with lenses.

If you are entertaining at home, appropriate space and light for formal and group shots tend to be more problematic. Existing light may need to be enhanced, and furniture may have to be moved or a room cleared, to accommodate a formal photo session. You will be wise to have the photographer see the space in advance. This will assure that he or she will have all necessary equipment on hand to produce the best possible results.

FOR EVERY OCCASION, A CAMERA

Many gatherings merit a camera, even Thanksgiving dinner at grandma's house, so consider these approaches as well:

◆ **DISPOSABLES.** A disposable camera operated by an amateur shutterbug will do at any event, large or small, if it's not possible to have or doesn't merit hiring a professional photographer. You should also consider giving guests disposable cameras, a popular practice at gatherings ranging from engagement parties, renewals of vows and weddings to baby showers, reunions and special anniversaries. The guests' shots can provide all the photos at an inexpensive affair or a very different record that supplements professional photography at grander celebrations.

◆ **DIGITALS.** The same holds for digital cameras. They are valuable tools for professionals, who can use them either as backup equipment, in case something happens to still cameras, or as primary equipment. With the digital, they can see immediately whether Aunt Harriet blinked or little Susie made a face and, if so, retake the shot. Moreover, digital photos, easily downloaded to a computer, can be sent swiftly to absent loved ones around the country and beyond, as well as to guests after the event. You can even set up a web site where family and friends can view the photographic record. (Your photographer may have a template you can use.) All this saves a lot of time and money in reproducing prints, and you don't have the hassle of mailing pictures to out-of-towners.

Digital cameras, though, are not just for professionals. Guests increasingly are toting them to a variety of celebrations. I know of one recent wedding, for example, at which some friends brought digital cameras. After several dozen shots of bride and groom and family and others were downloaded to a laptop, they were projected on a modest screen in one part of the hall, changing every five or 10 seconds, to the delight of those who viewed them (or were in them).

◆ **CAMCORDERS.** Many people use camcorders to create video records of children's birthdays, vacations and the like, and amateur use of these cameras also can be valuable at other gatherings, particularly less formal ones. At grander affairs, however, videography is best left to professionals. For one, it demands far too much of guests: They should not be expected to spend immense time recording individual interviews with all who want to offer congratulations, reminiscences or humorous remarks, a popular practice at many events. For another, serious videography requires special cameras and lighting, and it raises other challenges that are beyond the capacities of most amateurs. To wit:

VIDEOGRAPHY QUESTIONS

1. **NUMBER OF CAMERAS.** How many cameras, for example, will be used? The number clearly will affect the quality of the final product. Using just one camera will limit the perspectives and images that can be captured and the choices available in the editing process. Using two cameras will likely enrich the final tape significantly, making it less stiff, less predictable and more realistic.

2. **FORMAT.** Most often, video is best shot in BETA format. Copies can always be made in VHS. If the master is lost or destroyed, it may not be possible to get good copies from a VHS tape. You may also encounter poor reproduction if a VHS tape is to be projected on a large screen. BETA is generally more expensive, but it provides many more options than VHS, especially after the fact.

3. **SOUND.** Remember that the more individuals the videographer interviews, the more it will cost you. Beyond this, however, if the audio is going to record speeches, careful consideration should be given to those you choose to make remarks —and they should be advised in advance that the camera will be rolling. Not doing so can result in inarticulate comments or, worse, embarrassing ones.

It is also important to consider how natural sound—the background noise you can't control—will be used. In some instances it can enhance a tape, while in others it can be distracting. Houses of worship have varied policies on this. Some prohibit all sound equipment. Others let equipment pick up natural sound but not recorded sound such as wedding vows. Still others permit both. You should discuss this question carefully ahead of time with your videographer.

4. **SCRIPT.** Request a script-like document that the videographer will follow. It should include a short description of each frame and the accompanying natural or recorded sound. A script for a wedding, for instance, might look like the following:

Guests' arrival	Natural Sound
Designated seating *(Family Members)*	Natural Sound
Processional Attendants	Natural Sound
Bride & Father *(Before descending aisle)*	Recorded Sound
Musical Interlude	Natural Sound
Exchange of Vows	Recorded Sound

You also should consider recorded sound for speeches at retirements, anniversaries, birthdays and other celebrations. Recording accolades and good-natured roasts of the honorees will be a cherished reminder of good times and good fellowship. Whether you employ sound or not, however, this type of script can be a roadmap for any event you plan to put on videotape. If you don't have one, you may well end up with a disjointed film whose meaning is diminished. If a videographer should be reluctant to provide some documentation of the frames and/or sound bites, you would be wise to move on.

MEETING WITH PHOTOGRAPHERS OR VIDEOGRAPHERS

Once you narrow your search to two or three photographers or videographers, meet them at their place of business. That's where they will have work that has not been pre-selected for you, and you should ask to see some of it. Many people can take 10 great shots out of 200; you need someone of consistent quality and originality. So be relentless in your questions. Here, for example, are some concerns you should address:

◆ Ask to see proofs as well as finished photos of still photographers and unedited tapes and scripts of videographers.

◆ Make sure the person with whom you are meeting actually will do the work. If not, meet instead with the photographer to whom the job will be assigned. Otherwise you will be wasting your time.

◆ Be sure the photographer will have backup equipment. It's not uncommon for a flash or other lighting equipment or cameras to malfunction without warning.

◆ Discuss the photographer's definition of photojournalism if that is what you are after—and request sufficient examples of what he or she has done in this vein in the past.

◆ Be sure the photographer/videographer will have an assistant on hand. It's impossible for a photographer to perform his or her responsibilities and worry about details, too.

◆ Find out what type film and paper will be used—among other things, large prints can become grainy or out of focus, depending on film used in still photography—and, as noted, discuss BETA vs. VHS for videography.

◆ Many photographers and videographers have standard packages and prices from which to choose. Some include negatives, print proofs and master copies of videos. If these are not part of the package, ask how much it would cost to include them. If they are not for sale, ask if there is a time limit on when you can have copies made.

◆ Carefully consider the content of each package to be sure you don't jeopardize what you have envisioned as your final product. If the packages don't meet your expectations, ask the photographer to price your preferences.

◆ If the photographer you are meeting is a self-employed freelancer and has no colleagues, nail down—in writing—what would happen in the event of illness or other factors that might prevent him or her from showing up. Indeed, no matter who the photographer, be sure arrangements are made for comparable services in the event the person cannot fulfill his or her obligation.

◆ Many other items, of course, need to be detailed in a contract, from all services to be provided, hours of service and costs (including overtime) to payment schedules, a delivery timeline, cancellation policies and more. Lost images, for example, are impossible to replace, so acceptable compensation should be specified in the event film does not transport in the camera or is accidentally damaged later.

In the end, much will depend on your rapport with the photographer or videographer, so don't ignore any sign of discontent with a potential candidate. After your meetings and your reviews of their work and other items, moreover, you should ask for three references and check them out carefully. ◆

CHAPTER IX

Presentation Matters
(As Do Decorating and Rental Firms)

The world is governed more by appearance than realities . . .
— DANIEL WEBSTER

HOW THINGS LOOK is as important as—indeed, an integral part of—how things are. Those who consider this a superficial view should ask themselves why they don't yearn for an ugly spouse, hideous clothes or repellant food. Like it or not, presentation matters. That's why the road to successful celebrations is paved with decorating and rental firms. They are the foundation of the special events industry, and they can save you lots of grief.

What would you do, for example, if your spouse agreed to host a formal, seated dinner for 20 at your home—and you had china and crystal services for eight, no silverware to speak of, and your dining room table accommodated 10? Or consider another challenge: Your company is commemorating its 125th anniversary, and the chief executive officer wants to celebrate with 1,200 employees and clients at a luncheon—in a cavernous corporate warehouse that the CEO wants to look like a country home.

Such events can be pulled off with relative ease with the help of competent and well-stocked decorating and rental companies. Fortunately, there is no shortage of such firms in the Washington area. They can create site locations, design theme celebrations, transform unique or problem spaces and provide serving equipment and table décor fit for a king at a fraction of what it would cost you to buy it all.

WHAT'S FOR RENT?

As David Painter of Chantilly Event Rentals says, "If you can dream it, you can rent it." All sorts of facades, backdrops, paraphernalia and props can be rented to transport your guests anywhere in the world. Turn your event site into Paris, Rome or the foot of the U.S. Capitol. The location is up to you.

Consider a London landscape. With the help of decorating and rental firms, you can use fabrics, carpeting, wall and ceiling treatments, park benches, garden archways, lattice panels and Victorian street lamps to transport your guests to the center of London. Add complimentary table décor and service equipment, and even the most astute guest will envision being in Hyde Park!

Any atmosphere can be enhanced, moreover, with exquisite china, crystal and silver, which are available in just about every style and pattern imaginable. Carry a theme further with all sorts of table linens, from antique patterns to whimsical themed designs. Seat any number of guests at tables that come in various shapes and sizes and on several styles of chairs with matching cushions and covers. Whether you need to create or transform space with 10 plates and two tables or 300 tables and 3,000 chairs, everything and anything you need is available, and in styles to suit your

56

event and taste. The variety of table décor for rent is almost unlimited.

Attractive foliage also plays a major role in entertaining, not only as a decorating accent but also for transforming space. Foliage can be used to disguise unattractive views, make a room seem smaller, or create and divide space. It can brighten a nondescript stage or add sophistication to plain podiums. Greenery of all types can add balance to a color scheme or just the right touch to thematic decorations. Large or small, plants and trees add flair and enhance the atmosphere of any venue.

WHY RENT IT?

Why rent? If a celebration is to be held in a certain location regardless of its condition, or if the space has been chosen solely for sentimental reasons, you may need the help of a decorating company. Renting table décor is a lot less complicated but needs to be handled just as thoughtfully. Most hosts rent because they have insufficient quantities to serve all guests, but some also view renting as an opportunity to upgrade tableware and to vary styles, an area in which they can become quite creative. Organizers of one fundraising event I attended, for example, sectioned the dining room into quadrants, with tables in each quarter set in four styles—traditional, art deco, exotic and Victorian. The look was unexpected and smashing.

Stunning table linens add to your celebration's tone. Beautiful cloths made from damask, brocade and lace can significantly enhance more formal occasions, while twill, chintz or oilcloth can add to the atmosphere of garden parties or backyard buffets. Renting also affords the ability to change your décor and match it to the occasion. Successful companies constantly update their inventories to include the latest tabletop chic.

Renting, finally, can improve seating arrangements, especially if you are entertaining at home. Most of us have rectangular dining tables, the style best

suited to the dining rooms in our homes. But round tables bring guests closer together and enable more lively conversation. Everyone can be included. How many times have you wondered about the uproarious laughter coming from the far end of the table?

Think about renting chairs, too. You can seat more guests with rented chairs because they generally are not as large as the standard chairs of your dining room set. If your dinner is a formal one, consider renting Chivari chairs. They are attractive and come with a large selection of cushions and covers. If seating your table to capacity is your aim, you will be better off with standard wood folding chairs, which take up the least space and come in various finishes and colors. I would recommend, however, that you avoid plastic folding chairs. While they may be slightly less expensive to rent, they generally are unattractive and uncomfortable and can detract significantly from the overall ambience of the space in which they are used.

Most hotels have a limited selection of tableware. While I don't recommend renting china, glassware or silver for use at a hotel, you may want to consider renting an attractive base plate that adds color and panache to the setting.

Most hotels also have a limited selection of table linens. Standard colors might include white, cream, gray and perhaps pink, and the cloths can be drab. Should the hotel linens be unsatisfactory or detract from the look you are trying to achieve, consider renting a table topper or square overlay. Toppers or overlays are less expensive than entire cloths and can add the perfect dash of color or texture.

Whenever you rent linens, don't rely on a swatch from a sample book. While swatches can give you an idea of color and fabric, they can't let you see the entire pattern, which, when viewed in a whole cloth, may clash with aspects of your table décor or overall setting. So insist on seeing an actual cloth before you decide. I once selected a plaid cloth from a swatch. It showed the slightest bit of yellow stripe that seemed to provide the accent I wanted to achieve. When I saw the entire cloth, however, the yellow stripe dominated rather than highlighted the table décor. It looked awful. Seeing a full sample cloth will also help you avoid the disaster of using faded cloths that have been laundered excessively.

WHAT KIND OF FIRMS?

In general, decorating companies design themed events and transform space. They employ event specialists and designers who can advise you about any aspect of your celebration and will execute all or some of what needs to be done. They also rent location backdrops and props, carpeting, wall and ceiling treatments, tents and what I consider hardware—staging, platforms, flooring, staircases, lecterns and the like. Rental firms generally rent tableware, serving pieces, linens and what I consider software—barbecue grills, flower carts, popcorn machines and such. They also have professional staff members who can advise you about what's appropriate, what's hot, and what's been overused. Their expertise with regard to etiquette and the latest tabletop look is usually invaluable.

While these are the general distinctions between decorating and rental companies, there are exceptions to the rule. Some firms will provide a one-stop shopping experience, everything you need from planning to execution, if that's what you want. Others offer more specialized services, and still others limit service to one aspect of an event. Thus Hargrove, Inc. and Fandango are the two main decorating firms in the area that provide a broad array of services. D.C. Rental, Party Rentals and Perfect Settings are rental firms that concentrate mainly on tableware and software items. Companies like Gala Cloths specialize in linens, HDO in tents. You may decide to work with one of these companies or several, depending on your specific needs, taste and budget.

WHAT DOES IT COST?

Decorating and rental firms stock a wide array of props and equipment from which you can choose. The quality and quantity of what you pick obviously will affect your bill, but you can keep some costs in line if you are careful about your selections.

If you must transform space and decorate it, items like props, carpeting and wall and ceiling treatments will add considerably to expenses. It won't cost as much, though, if you choose items from a company's inventory rather than commissioning the firm to build or personalize what you want. Of course, you can create a facade depicting your favorite location, imprint your name and celebration date on base plates, monogram table linens or build a large thematic centerpiece, but you will be charged accordingly.

With table décor, it's a little like being in a candy store. You can rent some fabulous items, but choosing first this and then that adds up quickly. Bill Homan of Design Cuisine advises clients to spend on what guests will see. The base plate and glassware are generally the focal point of a seated meal, he says, so consider spending a little more on these items. Think carefully about linens as well. Patterned cloths or those made of fine silk or damask are beautiful, for instance, but they are generally more expensive than a plain linen cloth. (Also keep in mind that plain cloths won't fight with your choice of china, crystal and silver and that the design and fabric content of patterned cloths sometimes disappears when the table is completely set, especially in a large room with many tables.)

Whether you work with a decorating company, a rental company, a specialty company or all of them, be sure to check the items you receive well ahead of the scheduled party time. While the companies pride themselves on the quality of their wares, stained or torn linens or dirty dinnerware can be delivered undetected. Don't delay checking until it is too late to have the firm replace any problem items. ◆

CHAPTER X

Inviting Invitations

Of old all invitations ended
With the well-known R.S.V.P.,
But now our laws have been amended
The hostess writes B.Y.O.B.

— CHRISTOPHER MORLEY,
A Prohibition Verse

SOME INVITATIONS are formal and traditional, "the pleasure of your company" kind for weddings, bar and bat mitzvahs, debutante balls and other grand affairs. Others are less formal and more creative, including such things as special materials and graphic effects or snapshots for a milestone anniversary, special birthday, reunion or fundraiser. Still others are ready-made, available in shops for children's birthdays, baby showers and other occasions, with blanks to fill in or bordered space for writing or computer printing.

As for preparation, invitations can be engraved, printed, handwritten, handmade, computer-generated, ready-made or—heaven forbid—e-mailed (if you must use e-mails, please limit them to small, last-minute, casual get-togethers with close friends). Whatever invitation you extend, though, it should achieve three aims: (1) reflect the occasion's tone and meaning (2) convey all essential information, and (3) be, so to speak, inviting.

Whether or not Prohibition-era hostesses asked guests to bring their own bottles, for example, some people do like to get inventive with invitations. Sometimes this can provide a breath of fresh air. At other times, however, it can go too far, as with this invitation that I learned about from David Painter of Chantilly Event Rentals in Virginia:

> YO!
>
> IT'S A WEDDING
>
> BE THERE
>
> NAMES OF THE COUPLE
>
> DATE
>
> TIME
>
> PLACE
>
> **Let us know or else**
> **Phone Number**

That violates aims 1 and 3: The tone and meaning of marriage have nothing to do with being a smart aleck, which isn't exactly an inviting attitude, either. A student might get away with a "Yo, Be There" invitation for a casual classmates' gathering. It is out of line, however, for a wedding, which usually calls for the most formal of invitations. Even the "Yo" invitation, though, did have a sense of essential information. All formal invitations, for example, should conform, at a minimum, to the following information format:

> *Host Line*
>
> *Request Line*
>
> *Event Line*
>
> *Date Line*
>
> *Time Line*
>
> *Place Line*

They also should state the dress code and other information specific to your celebration. Will there be valet parking? Is it a surprise party, requiring everyone to show up at a certain time to help pull it off? For a wedding, will the reception after the ceremony be at the same site or elsewhere? When you end with that R.S.V.P. line, you also are likely to add not B.Y.O.B. but "Reply Card Enclosed" and include something like:

> *Mr. and Mrs.* _____
>
> *Accept* ___ /*Regretfully Decline* ___
>
> *The kind invitation of*
>
> *Mr. and Mrs.* _____
>
> *To the wedding of their daughter Mary*
>
> *to*
>
> *Mr. Paul Brown*
>
> *Monday, July 16, at five o'clock*

Printed reply cards, accompanied by stamped return envelopes, now almost always take the place of what used to be the courteous way to respond to a formal invitation: a handwritten note on personal stationery. In today's rushed world, the reply card, which does speed the response process, has become the norm, at least for formal invitations. The one problem with them is that invitees sometimes forget to fill in their names. The tendency is to mark "Accept" or "Regret" and mail the card back, so the host or hostess has no notion of which people, or exactly how many, will be attending. You can solve this problem by assigning numbers to all invitees on your list and placing each one's number on the back of the reply card sent with the invitation. If guest number 24 sends back a card marked "Accept" but omits names, the number will tell you who it is. It takes a little extra time, but it will be time well spent.

With the invitation itself, the host and request lines cause the most awkwardness for people, particularly with invitations to weddings that are hosted and financed by a group of people, such as divorced parents and stepparents. Wording for second wedding invitations also makes some people cringe. That's silly. Depending on circumstances, invitations for second marriages can be as formal as others or as informal as you like. Generally speaking, unless your spouse-to-be has never been married, it is probably wiser to go the informal route. As for formal second-wedding invitations, they do follow certain etiquette, and most stationers should be able to assist on wording for one (as well as on how to handle a group of hosts). Whatever the situation, think about what makes sense. Common courtesy and good manners never go out of style.

Nor does the most personal kind of invitation—a warm, handwritten note. It is especially appropriate and feasible if you are inviting fewer than 50 guests, whether to a 25th anniversary celebration, a 6th or 60th birthday party or a wedding. In fact, many brides choose handwritten invitations, particularly if the marriage involves a civil ceremony.

No matter what kind of invitation you prefer, though, each individual (as well as married couples, of course) should receive one. If you have single friends with significant others or someone else they wish to accompany them, their guests should receive individual invitations. You should not extend an invitation to "Ms. Mary Brown and Guest." Not only does it make the guest feel insignificant, but unless Mary Brown includes the name of her guest on the response card, you could have a seating problem. While some think you create a "gift problem" by issuing a separate invitation to a single friend's guest, I disagree. Single people attending an event as a couple should make no assumptions about gifts. A conversation about what's appropriate will solve any "problem."

MAKING THEM INVITING

The appeal of invitations is affected by a number of questions. Some examples:

◆ **PRINTING AND PAPER QUALITY.** Relatively few people today have invitations engraved, a time-consuming and expensive process involving an etched plate that results in raised lettering. Instead, more and more people use thermography, a swifter and less costly raised-lettering process in which powder is fused by heat to fresh ink. Thermography, which is entirely acceptable today, produces lovely invitations (as well as response cards, reception cards, thank-you cards and other items), so you need not spend that extra money to get attractive results. Thermography also has an additional benefit: The money you save makes it possible to afford better-quality paper, which definitely adds to an invitation's appeal.

◆ **ENVELOPES.** With the improved paper come equally good envelopes in which to encase the invitation package. With formal invitations,

especially for weddings, double envelopes often are used—an outer, or mailing, envelope and an inner envelope, which frequently is lined with fabric or special paper. The two-envelope tradition began as a way to ensure that invitees received clean and crisp invitations that were not stained or marked during the mailing process. Though they are not required, double envelopes add an elegant touch (as does tissue paper with formal invitations). They also add another budget line—atop the cost of the extra outer envelopes that you should order to accommodate addressing mistakes (10 extra for every 50 invitations should be more than sufficient.) Also, be sure to take formal invitations, with all enclosures, to the post office ahead of time to check stamp needs; the weight or shape of some invitations may require additional postage.

◆ **CALLIGRAPHY.** Opening a high-quality invitation that is beautifully addressed with calligraphy is a satisfying, even exciting, experience. It is, of course, costly to have envelope addresses, return addresses and reply cards done by a calligrapher. If you can afford it, however, it adds a lovely touch, especially in the hands of someone like Caren Milman of Caren Milman Calligraphy in Rockville, Maryland, one of several fine calligraphers in the area.

If your budget won't allow for the real thing, you can have calligraphy done less expensively by machine. For example, Mary Derderian at Wrap It Up in Vienna, Virginia—and stationers don't come much better than Derderian, who is a former president of the Association of Wedding Professionals—provides this service (as do some others), using a robotic system designed by two MIT students. It looks like a flat lettering bed with an attached fountain pen. The pen—which Derderian calls "Jane"—mimics the hand to create a beautiful look of fine calligraphy. "Jane," she says, can address about 15 envelope sets an hour, or write about 12 invitations or 30 escort/seating cards an hour, in many ink colors beyond the traditional black. If you prefer another type of machine for such work, you can easily find software and vendors to produce computer calligraphy.

◆ **CUSTOM-DESIGNED INVITATIONS.** If money is no object, custom-designed invitations, usually created by graphic artists, can have a forceful impact on your affair. These can be simple or complex works. Some might have four or eight folds, so that they open like a brochure to some surprise within. Others might have three-dimensional graphics or musical effects. Many enticing things can be done if you have the budget, the right designer or stationer, the right printer and enough lead-time.

◆ **HANDMADE INVITATIONS.** Handmade invitations, particularly those you make yourself, send a very special message. Not only because you've designed the look, used graphics and pictures to create excitement, added color, or expressed your enthusiasm in verse, rhyme or poetry. Or because you created different effects with papers, a computer, ribbons or other home tools. It's simply because the very act of making the invita-

tions yourself speaks volumes, saying how much you care about the event or the honoree or the family members or old friends invited to a celebration. However, making your own invitations takes time and money (depending on the supplies you select) and often requires the help of others. So they work best when the guest list is relatively small, when you plan well ahead, and when others are willing to pitch in.

If you are unsure about the wording, etiquette or other aspects of invitations, it is easy to check out such matters. An event planner, if you are using one, should have all the answers, and she or he also can bring you invitation samples from which to choose. Alternatively, you can consult with Washington-area stationers, from Premier Printing & Services of Washington (which provides consultation and service in your home) to the Washington office of Baltimore-based Bethesda Engravers (which has counted the President and other eminent figures among its clients) to Creative Parties in Bethesda, Maryland (which provides a wide array of in-stock and custom-made invitations) to Wrap It Up and others. You also can check out some of their web sites *(See directory on p. 108)* and those of other invitation suppliers nationally.

Finally, if you are in a hurry to have invitations printed, American Printing Company in Cheverly, Maryland, excels at quick turnarounds.   ◆

CHAPTER XI

Eating Your Cake
(And Having It, too)

*You know you are getting old when
the candles cost more than the cake.*

— BOB HOPE

ALTHOUGH MARIE ANTOINETTE, the infamous wife of France's King Louis XVI, never actually said, "Let them eat cake," some Washington-area bakers regard it as a good idea. They consider it effective marketing to let potential customers eat cake before deciding whether to have it for their event. Creative Cakes of Silver Spring, Maryland, for example, holds tastings one Sunday afternoon a month (except in December), with the specific dates posted on its web site. *(See Directory on pp. 97, 98.)*

The practice works well for both bakers and customers. Bakers can reach many of those who need the cakes that are central to weddings, birthdays, anniversaries, construction topping-out ceremonies (which originated in medieval times to appease the gods of trees cut down for buildings), christenings, bar or bat mitzvahs and many other occasions. Customers, for their part, can see and sample many cake options with no pressure to buy.

Bakeries that offer regularly scheduled tastings tend to be larger commercial firms. Smaller bakeries or boutique bakers offer tastings, too, but these usually are by appointment, and samples are more limited. Which type of baker you select will depend on your event, your preferences and your budget. Smaller bakeries can spend more time discussing your requirements, and boutique bakers will design and produce one-off creations especially for your occasion.

Smallwood Bakers of Waldorf, Maryland, for one, specializes in novelty and wedding cakes, and it will arrange a tasting according to your specifications. For instance, you can sample one chocolate and one vanilla cake, each laced with different fillings. Tastings are held every Saturday between 10 a.m. and 5 p.m. or at other times by appointment.

At Victorian Cakes in Fairfax Station, Virginia, you will be invited to taste a slice of only one flavor, buttered vanilla cake with a touch of almond. However, you also will be interviewed about your personal taste and sense of style to determine the design, type and flavor of cake best suited for you—including a musical one that will play your favorite tune, if you wish. Owner Grace Holland, who hails from Peru, says that in South America cakes imply a person's stature. Therefore, "You cannot have a la-la cake (translation: so-so cake.) It has to be sensational. You must show your style. And the cake must be a testament to your emotions."

Heidelberg Pastry Shoppe in Arlington, Virginia, is

an excellent commercial baker. While you can be assured that you will receive the yummiest of cakes, you will select it from a book containing set designs. No formal Heidelberg tastings are held, but you can speak with a baker who periodically "holds court" at their sample table.

Cakes can be had in almost endless varieties. As Mark Ramsdell, Director of Professional Pastry Programs at L'Academie Cuisine, says, "If you can think it, we can bake it."

SHAPES AND SIZES

You can get tiered cakes, heart-shaped cakes, square cakes or rectangular sheet cakes. Rounds, because they symbolize an unbroken circle, are especially popular for weddings. There are tall cakes and small, individual cakes, cakes with a combination of forms and cakes made in special shapes to celebrate whatever occasion you choose. For just a few examples, numeral cutouts make a perfect milestone anniversary cake, a hammer-shaped creation will honor the handyman you married who just refinished the basement, and an edible champagne bottle embedded in the center of a cake can add the right touch to most celebrations.

Cakes for kids' parties also can be made to resemble numerous objects in kids' lives— soccer fields, cartoon characters, Teddy bears, ballet dancers, racing cars or whatever—as can concoctions for reunions, neighborhood street parties or business affairs. Susan Thurston, owner of The Cakery, for example, specializes in two- and three-dimensional cakes that are particularly popular with companies celebrating anniversaries or new facilities. Containing all of the necessary supports—you do not want an elaborate cake to crumble, so to speak, because of music

vibrations or other factors—the cakes are constructed from blueprints and artists' renderings.

INGREDIENTS

Ingredients are almost as varied as shapes. You can pick chocolate, passion fruit or soursop, almond, vanilla, mocha, rum, fruit—just about any flavor you can imagine. Your choice of icings usually includes butter cream, whipped cream and fondant, and the icing can be flavored however you prefer.

DECORATIONS

Decorating options may be the most numerous of all. For some examples:

◆ Hand-made and sugar-blown decorations as well as fresh flowers work well, especially for wedding cakes. If you decide to use flowers, check on whose responsibility it is to order them, yours or the baker's (and make sure that the flowers are not poisonous).

◆ Computers have made their mark in the world of cakes. It is now possible to decorate a cake with an edible reproduction of just about any image, whether a likeness of the guest of honor, a picture of a company's new headquarters or an architectural rendering of your new house.

◆ Little trinkets artistically placed atop a cake can delight children, as can cakes with items baked into them. You must be especially careful, however, that no solid items are inadvertently swallowed. Kids love to find prizes in their portions, and in such cases the baker should tell the server exactly where the prizes are, and the children must be told to look for prizes first with a fork. Would-be grooms who are anxious about popping the question also have been known to have an engagement ring baked into a cake. They, too, would be well advised to tell their ladies to look for something before taking a bite, lest the ring not end up on her finger.

◆ Family heirlooms, fabrics, statuary or unique bride-and-groom cake toppers all can be used as decorations. The original cake topper from a long-ago wedding cake can't be beaten for a 25th or 50th anniversary cake, and a swatch from a child's security blanket can provide a nice touch on, say, a 21st birthday cake.

◆ The possibilities for a groom's cake, primarily a Southern tradition, are also endless. These cakes, first used to offer guests an alternative to the bride's (white) cake, usually were a chocolate confection. Nowadays, they generally are served at bachelor parties (though they can be used at any celebration honoring the groom), and they tend to reflect the groom's personality. The cake for one groom I was told about was baked and decorated like a giant Ho-Ho, the groom's favorite childhood snack. Superman, Batman and Spiderman are popular, too, but you should be aware that many bakers will not reproduce registered, trademarked or copyrighted designs.

SPECIAL REQUIREMENTS

For those on restricted diets, a number of bakers can meet your special needs. Victorian Cakes, for example, makes satisfying creations for diabetics. (It also makes cholesterol-free cakes, and if you require ingredients that use no animal products, it can steer you to such cakes as well.) Owner Grace Holland, who is a diabetic, says she began making sugar-free cakes because she felt sorry for diabetic children who were unable to eat regular birthday

cakes. So as not to embarrass the kids (or adults), she makes a sugar-free top tier for the diabetics. Only the hostess or host knows the difference and serves applicable slices to guests.

For those with other medical conditions, not to mention chocoholics, a flourless chocolate mousse cake can be ordered from The Cakery. And although not available on a regular basis, The Cakery's Thurston also will prepare wheatless, lactose-free or gluten-free cakes if you provide the recipe. Caterers, such as Design Cuisine, will do the same, but "ingredients are expensive," said owner Bill Homan, "and that will be reflected in the cost of a special cake."

COSTS

Prices for cakes, in fact, range widely, from inexpensive birthday cakes at neighborhood pastry shops or ice cream parlors to extravagant inventions costing hefty sums. You can pay tens of thousands of dollars, for example, for an elaborate, 7-foot creation by Sylvia Weinstock, and clients are willing to pay for her creativity, her handwork and her experience. But the acclaimed New York baker also produces smaller and less expensive original designs. Weinstock says, "We're an affordable luxury."

Locally, Narcisa Vieira-Castillo, the former Ritz Carlton and Willard Hotel pastry chef who runs Cakes Unique, will produce original creations, too. Castillo, who specializes in wedding cakes, says, "Cake baking is as much art as any other artistic endeavor." So if you select a customized cake, baked to your specifications, expect to pay top dollar. Cakes from larger commercial bakeries will cost somewhat less.

A CAKE CHECKLIST

Here is the kind of checklist you should have in choosing a cake for your celebration:

◆ Eat cake at at least two tastings (perhaps one at a larger commercial house, another at a custom baker) before deciding which creation you will have at your affair.

◆ Ask if the baker will prepare a show cake. Show cakes are just that, meant for show. They are served to a relative handful of guests, while all others get slices from a sheet cake in the kitchen. This can result in sizable savings.

◆ Be sure the cake is made from scratch, and check on the ingredients to be used for both the cake and the icing. (The icing color—white vs. off-white—can be affected by ingredient choices.)

◆ When will the cake be prepared? Will it be frozen? Will the ingredients hold up in warm weather?

◆ Will the cake's structure support the proposed decorations and stand up to any vibrations such as those caused by music or dancing?

◆ Will someone be available at the celebration site to make any last-minute adjustments or repairs to the cake?

◆ How and when will the cake be delivered? Will there be a separate delivery charge? Will the cake be transported in a refrigerated vehicle?

◆ Does the baker prepare individual table cakes that can be used as centerpieces as well as dessert?

◆ Will you be charged for the traditional anniversary top tier on a wedding cake? Many bakers provide it at no cost or at least offer a discount. The tier is generally removed and packaged for freezing so that you can enjoy it on your first wedding anniversary.

◆ Check the baker's credentials, references and whether the local/state health department licenses him or her.

If you choose not to eat cake, Bundles of Cookies offers a number of creatively designed and customized alternatives for just about any celebration.   ◆

CHAPTER XII

Partying Under a Tent

*In the spring I have counted 136 different kinds
of weather inside of 24 hours.*

—MARK TWAIN,
New England Weather speech

MARK TWAIN'S NEW ENGLAND was not the only place with weather volatility. The old Washington cliché about the weather—that if you don't like it, wait 15 minutes and it will change—is fairly accurate as well. Regardless of the season, the sun can be shining one minute, the sky dumping buckets of rain the next. Thunderstorms come out of nowhere, and blustery winds descend in seconds. It can be hot in February and freezing in September. In an interview with *Washington Post* reporter Roxanne Roberts, event planner Anne Fleming said that when she works on an event involving outside space, she closes her eyes, envisions the worst and plans from there. Smart lady.

So if any part of your event is to be held outdoors, your anti-disaster planning should start with a tent, a decision that should not be made at the last minute. While tent companies will go to great lengths to help clients shelter guests against the elements, they can't turn on a dime. They will need some notice to have sufficient personnel on hand for the job and to ensure that the ground beneath the tent is dry and stays that way.

You can, of course, include tents in your plans for aesthetic reasons as well, since there is virtually no limit to the environments that can be created beneath them (*See What Goes Underneath on p. 68*). Most of us, however, will simply want to avoid soaking-wet guests and food. Yes, having such shel-ter will put a dent in your budget, but cheap is dear, as my grandmother used to say. If your budget won't allow for a tent, you should consider another venue or limit guests to those who can be accommodated inside.

The Washington area has its share of excellent firms to meet your outdoor needs. Mike Graves, vice president of HDO Productions, says the best ones provide more than just a structure. "That includes the actual shelter to be used, heating or cooling if necessary, and related utilities such as lighting and flooring."

STYLES OF SHELTER

You can choose from three main tent designs—pole, frame or structure. Each type has its pluses and minuses, and, as Graves says, "Whether the specific characteristics are an advantage or disadvantage is often in the eye of the beholder." Pole tents have interior poles that support and help shape the tent. Frame tents are made with an interior frame, usually 2-inch tubular aluminum, with the tent top stretched over the frame and attached to it. Both designs are anchored with ropes. Structure tents are essentially larger frame tents, using aluminum box beams to make rafters and the like.

POLE TENTS, generally the least expensive, usually start at 20 feet x 20 feet and go up to 150 feet wide and as long as needed or available. Most often they require inflexible positioning ground anchors and have more side poles than a frame or structure tent, but they usually have higher ceilings and no ceiling obstructions or hardware.

FRAME TENTS, which are slightly more expensive, have ceilings with extensive interior framework, usually requiring use of a ceiling liner. The size of a frame tent is a bit more restrictive, ranging from 10 feet x 10 feet and going up to 50 feet wide and as long as needed or available. But there are no interior poles to work around, and anchoring is flexible. They can even be anchored by ballast weights and can go just about anywhere, including against a building to provide seamless passage between indoors and outdoors.

STRUCTURE TENTS are the most expensive. They range in size from 10 feet x 10 feet to what Graves describes as "the big daddy"—164 feet by however long is necessary or available. In general, they offer a more aesthetic-looking ceiling and 13-foot to 15-foot side heights (as opposed to the usual 10-foot side heights of other tents). No ropes are used to secure a structure tent, but each "leg" must be firmly anchored to something. In addition, these tents offer a higher degree of structural strength.

The size tent needed is determined by the number of square feet required to accommodate guests, seating, food tables, catering/service kitchens, musicians and (if you are having one) a dance floor. A preset formula is used to calculate total square footage as well as the space required to conform to fire and safety regulations. (*See accompanying guide to calculate the size tent you may need*).

Whichever style you choose will be determined by your specific needs. Just check that the vendor has contacted authorities to make sure that there are no restrictions on grounding the tent.

WHAT GOES UNDERNEATH

Tents can have all sorts of looks and accessories. They come in colors and stripes. They can have side panels, either clear or opaque, that are handy for keeping out rain and drafts. Some side panels even mimic palladium windows and include French doors. Many ceiling treatments also are available, the most popular being ceiling liners. They come in various

---

A Tent Size Guide

A GUIDE TO FIGURING REQUIRED TENT SIZES

Actual dimensions can vary, but in general tent sizes start at 10 feet x 10 feet, with both length and width increasing in 10-foot increments. The following table, courtesy of Sugarplum Tents, provides a guide to the size tents needed for up to 300 guests.

No. of Guests	Seated at Tables	Standing or Buffet
50	20' x 40'	20' x 30'
100	30' x 50'	30' x 30'
150	40' x 60'	40' x 40'
200	40' x 80'	40' x 60'
250	60' x 70'	40' x 80'
300	60' x 80'	60' x 60'

These calculations do not include stages, dance floors, catering kitchens or serving tables. (Also, please remember when sizing tents to allow enough space for everyone to be covered in case of inclement weather.)

fabrics and colors and can add dramatically to any décor. When First Lady Jackie Kennedy hosted a dinner at Mount Vernon in July 1963 for the president of Pakistan, for example, she used a lovely turquoise tent with a soft yellow ceiling liner. A replica of that tent was made by HDO Productions for a fundraising dinner for Mt. Vernon at which the entire evening Mrs. Kennedy planned in 1963 was recreated. It was a sensational event, made more special by the stunning tent. Other choices for what to put beneath the tent, in addition to guests, food and music:

DECORATIVE ITEMS

The atmosphere beneath a tent can be enhanced with dramatic ceiling fans, with candelabras and with floral arrangements hung from the ceiling and from tent poles in all sorts of stylish containers or in open, moss-filled baskets. An experienced tent company will have a wealth of ideas to help you transform ordinary space beneath a tent into everything from a beautiful garden to an Italian country inn.

EXTRA LIGHTING

Most tent companies provide basic lighting for an evening event, but there's much to be said for using lighting for more than the basics, even though it may be expensive. Special lighting can enhance a romantic atmosphere or create just the right mood. Your tent company can contract with a lighting house, or you may wish to hire one directly. Either way, you sometimes can achieve more with lighting than with contrived decorations. The lighting may also require the use of a generator, which can be noisy. Should one be needed, be sure that it won't drown out your program or your guests' conversation.

HEATING AND COOLING

Tents can be heated or cooled, although about 60 percent of all events in tents need no climate control. It's cheaper to heat a tent than to cool one. While propane gas units are best to heat with, electrical units are available at venues where propane is prohibited. The cost is determined by many variables, including the shelter's square footage, the number of guests and the temperature. New air conditioning units also have built-in electric heating units, making set-up and climate control easier in unpredictable situations. Temperatures permitting, you can forgo air conditioning and use ceiling fans. While pedestal fans are said to be effective and less expensive, they are ugly, noisy and uncomfortable, often blowing hot air into guests' faces. Ceiling fans also offer aesthetic opportunities that pedestal fans do not. Local jurisdictions generally require permits for climate control, so be sure your tent company applies for proper permission.

FLOORING

Most tents are erected over existing surfaces—patios or grass. However, if the ground is too rough or affected by water, or if the grass tends to get soggy or cold, you may want to install special flooring. This can include, for example, turf carpet on bare ground or grass, plywood sub-flooring beneath the turf carpet or a raised and leveled floor covered with turf carpet.

DANCE FLOORS

If your tent is over ground or grass and the event includes dancing, a dance floor is a must. Some companies have standard floors that can be installed, but you can also arrange for customized floors done up in all sorts of designs and colors. They are beautiful, but expect to pay for the luxury. ◆

CHAPTER XIII

Riding to a Dream

But get me to the church on time.

—ALAN JAY LERNER AND FREDERICK LOWE,
My Fair Lady

WHEN MOST PEOPLE THINK about transportation for celebrations, and particularly weddings, the first thing that comes to mind is a sleek standard limousine for the bridal party or a minivan to shuttle guests from the hotel to the wedding to the reception and back. Others use more unusual transportation, including horse-drawn carriages for the couple and their parents and grandparents, a trolley-bus for shuttling guests, or a Rolls Royce or antique car for the bridal party. Whatever your inclination, however, it's important to look beyond the glamour and romance of the transportation to some practical matters.

In the joy of the moment, it may be hard to do this. But arriving at your wedding in the middle of a driving rain atop a roofless, horse-drawn carriage, for example, is not an especially good idea. So you will want assurances that the company has suitable, last-minute replacements for any vehicles you choose, especially if the vehicle suffers a mechanical failure. Being stuck in a broken limo on your wedding day also is not fun. There are, in fact, a variety of practical matters to attend to if you use motorized vehicles, whether for a wedding, a prom, a family reunion, a funeral or other occasions. Here are the foremost to consider:

♦ **SAFETY.** Safety, which should be the principal concern of any transportation company, is non-negotiable. Qualified, licensed drivers who have been properly trained, who are drug-free and who operate properly maintained vehicles are a must.

♦ **INSURANCE.** The company's policy should name you as an additional insured, to protect you from being sued in case of accident or injury. The odds, of course, are overwhelmingly against you getting into an accident, but that is no reason for you to forgo this protection.

♦ **CROSS-JURISDICTION LICENSING.** If you are traveling, for example, between the District of Columbia and Virginia, the transportation company should be licensed to operate between the jurisdictions. (Any questions you may have about jurisdictional licensing can be answered by your local taxi cab commission.)

♦ **ROUTES.** Make sure that the driver knows where he or she is going, the best way to get there and how to avoid traffic. You do not want to spend your special day giving directions to a driver. (Remember all those drivers who didn't know how to get you to the airport or back home?)

♦ **DRESS AND MANNERS.** The driver also needs to be properly attired. Limousine drivers usually dress as chauffeurs in a dark suit, tie and cap or a tuxedo, depending on your preference. Van or bus drivers should be uniformed, but usually are not, so be sure to determine in advance what bus drivers will be wearing and that his or her attire is acceptable to you. All drivers should be well groomed and well mannered. Grumpy bus drivers do not make for happy guests.

◆ **FLEXIBILITY.** Be sure to check on the flexibility of the driver and of the vehicle's availability. If you want to make an unscheduled stop at the last moment, will the driver accommodate such a request? Sometimes you find out too late that he or she will not deviate from the schedule as originally planned. Similarly, be sure to inquire if the vehicle is available beyond the contract time. Let's say you rent a vehicle between noon and 4:00 p.m. What happens if things run late and you need the car or bus until 4:30? If it's been contracted to someone else beginning at 5:00, you're probably out of luck.

Any good transportation company should be able to satisfy all such needs, and you should not hesitate to ask to see proper credentials for drivers and vehicles as well as insurance policies and riders. Once these issues have been resolved to your satisfaction, you're ready to move on to the next tier of concerns.

The number and size of vehicles needed, as well as other personal preferences, must be determined before you can begin to discuss costs. What style vehicle do you want? Would you like snacks and beverages? (Some companies may not provide alcohol.) Are mirrors, mood lighting and tinted glass important to you? All such frills add to the cost. Other extras might include bilingual drivers or security personnel.

Marty Janis, a veteran transportation consultant who is president of Atlantic Services Group, Inc., rightly stresses that transportation creates the first and last impression of an event, so who and what you select warrants careful consideration.

TRADITIONAL VEHICLES

In deciding on vehicles for celebrations, your choice should be based in part on the number of anticipated passengers. Town Car sedans, for example, are perfect for three or four people. Limousines can accommodate six, eight or 10 passengers. (The largest limo usually is a white stretch.) Vans and minivans can transport between 13 and 37 people and can be configured to accommodate different numbers of guests. Executive coaches or "party buses," as they are sometimes called, can accommodate 16 to 20 passengers, while motor coaches can seat 47 or 57.

Prices vary, as do minimums, depending on vehicle size and season. Additional fees are also charged for the time needed for the vehicle to travel from and to its garage, known as "drive time." In May or June, you can count on four-hour to six-hour minimums on these vehicles. This is an extremely busy time for transportation companies due to weddings and proms. For proms, in fact, minimums for limousines often increase to eight to 10 hours from the usual four hours.

Most companies have competitive rates, but you should check several operators for the best prices. Many companies have wedding packages, but not all offer discounts for volume use. Special prices also may be available if a transportation company has a special working arrangement with the venue that you select for your celebration. Some hotels also will provide transportation to a particular venue at no cost as part of their package for group room bookings. If you're using a hotel for family and friends, be sure to check on this before contracting with a transportation company. If you wish, transportation companies also will provide drivers to transport you in your own vehicles.

UNIQUE VEHICLES

If you are inclined to employ a novel vehicle, you should take into account potential pitfalls. Is the vehicle equipped with heating and/or air conditioning? If not, do you care if, in cold weather, a bride might have to don a heavy coat that could crush her wedding dress or if, in warm weather, her hairdo might droop in the humidity? Is the vehicle capable of traveling the necessary distance and arriving at your destination on time? Should there be a breakdown, are there sufficient and acceptable replacement vehicles, and will they travel along with the antique or classic car you've hired, just in case? Classic autos can add glamour and excitement, but it is wise to be realistic about them and prepare for the worst.

Many novel vehicles can be used and are available from several reputable firms. Alabaster's of Virginia has a fleet of vintage Rolls Royce Silver Clouds, while at Regal Limousine Service, also based in Virginia, you can hire a Bentley (both companies provide area-wide service). Midge Harmon of Harmon Carriages in Virginia, rents horse-drawn carriages.

Antique cars are also available, as are even more unusual modes of transportation. I know of one groom, a professional fire fighter, for example, who arranged for an antique fire engine to transport him and his bride to the fire hall where they were hosting their reception.

Some vehicles also can be used for more than one purpose. My friend Val LoCascio, for example, used a motorized trolley to transport her and her new husband, along with wedding guests, from the church to the reception site. The trolley, she said, not only added to the festivity of the day but also served as the receiving line after the church ceremony. The couple greeted each guest as they boarded. "It was efficient and fun," she said. Another dual-use vehicle: Executive coaches or party buses can be used for sightseeing vehicles for out-of-town family and friends or to transport guests between restaurants for a "progressive" dinner—appetizers at one watering hole, entrée at another, dessert at a third—in celebration of a milestone birthday or special anniversary.

VALET PARKING OR SHUTTLE BUS?

Trying to find a parking spot, whether for a formal affair or a home event, can sometimes be irritating, especially in heavy-traffic areas. Many people, therefore, provide valet parking to help make the occasion more pleasant and elegant. Fewer, however, seem aware of the value of offering shuttle transportation instead for local guests as well as for out-of-towners staying in hotels.

Janis, for example, says that a shuttle service works very well for all kinds of celebrations, including kids' parties and weddings. If your affair is at a venue that might be congested at the time of the celebration, local guests can park at a central parking lot and be transported to and from the event. In Georgetown or anywhere downtown, for instance, parking spaces can be few and far between. That means it takes longer to park a car, requiring the use of more valets. It also means guests have to wait, sometimes too long, to retrieve their vehicles.

Janis adds, "Sometime I just refuse to do valet parking. We have our reputation to think about, and most guests don't stop to think about the difficulty involved in parking and retrieving cars. All they know is they have to wait, and that doesn't reflect well on Atlantic."

In most cases, moreover, a shuttle is less costly. You pay a flat fee to rent the garage or lot, which Janis says is a pass-through charge, not one from which the transportation company profits. The firm's fees are based on the costs of the shuttle vehicles and the services of two or three traffic directors. These professionals are stationed at the event site and in the parking garage to assist guests.

Valet parking fees will depend on location, which will, among other things, determine the number of valets required. There's no doubt, though, that valet parking can be a more expensive and less convenient option. ◆

CHAPTER XIV

Walking Down the Aisle

I talk marriage; they talk weddings!

— ROBERT FARRAR CAPON,
On counseling engaged couples

SOME FEMALES begin planning their weddings as little girls. Others, both men and women, dwell on the matter only after the fateful decision has been made. Still others shudder at the thought of ever putting it all together. Whatever your predisposition, though, the wedding holds a central place among celebrations, the party of parties, and is therefore deserving of special attention.

Many things should be abundantly clear from all that has come before in this book, particularly the fact that while a wedding is about love, trust and lifetime commitment, planning it is an exercise in endurance, minutia and diplomacy. Only the well-versed and astute will survive with their trains and boutonnieres intact, their family relationships and friendships strong, and their memories cherished.

Most of what you need to know about weddings has appeared in previous chapters—on magical, Washington-area settings for your nuptials, on holding your affair in your home or in a faraway land, on caterers, musicians, florists, photographers and others who will be involved. For example, I have tried to make it clear that with vendors, the first among equals is the party planner, that the best plan is to hire somebody else to do a great deal of the work. This does not mean, of course, that you will then have nothing to do yourself, only that you will endure far less stress both during the planning and at the celebration itself, no small benefit.

In addition to what has already been explained, however, some matters are specific to weddings alone, from choosing a wedding gown to picking a honeymoon spot to dealing with two sets of families and the complications that this can cause for guest lists, venues and other questions. Indeed, the very complexity of a traditional wedding, with a rehearsal dinner beforehand, a brunch afterward and endless details in between, requires a plan, complete with budget, checklist and timeline, that is far more extensive than any made for other celebrations.

The planning process usually starts at least a year in advance of the wedding. This is when you should hire a wedding planner if you intend to do so—and have that person map out that master plan for you. Then you should (1) pick potential dates for the big day, (2) start choosing your wedding party and (3) begin looking for a wedding dress.

1. **PICKING THREE DATES.** It is important to pick three potential dates, lest your first choices for a ceremony site, reception venue and caterer are unavailable. It's no secret that many couples want to wed on three-day holiday weekends, to accommodate out-of-town guests as well as the pre-wedding rehearsal dinner and the post-wedding brunch. So if that is your preference, the sooner you start checking out dates the better,

coordinating all the while with both of the families involved and with the main attendants. This means moving toward booking your house of worship or other appropriate venue, your officiant, your reception venue (if it is to be in a different location) and your caterer (if the reception site does not provide food service).

2. **CHANGING CHOICES FOR WEDDING PARTIES.** You and your intended should then select attendants and others for your wedding party, keeping in mind that much has been changing in this area. Today, if a groom wants to have, say, a sister as his witness, a "best woman" is sometimes selected instead of a best man. For similar reasons, some brides choose to have a "man of honor" instead of a maid or matron of honor, and they even occasionally substitute "bridesmen" for bridesmaids.

In some cases, children from former marriages are picked for these roles, one of several ways in which couples are wisely including them in second-wedding ceremonies. For example, Val LoCascio married a widower who had a five-year old daughter. They called upon the child, Gabriela Walker, to join them at the altar for the exchange of rings. After Val and Brad exchanged their rings, they placed one on Gabriela's hand to signify their new family. It was quite moving.

Gabriela also participated in the lighting of the unity candle, a task more often given to the mothers of the bride and groom, which is one way to provide parents with greater involvement in church ceremonies. Often before ushers seat the mothers, they take them to light two smaller candles. The bride and groom then use those candles to light the central unity candle, signifying the union of the families as well as the couple. In other ceremonies, the mothers jointly light the unity candle, which the bride and groom then use to light alter candles. Some observers also recommend that when more than one child from an earlier marriage is involved, a

lighting be done at the reception, with the children using a unity candle to light additional candles. This is another way to recognize them individually and as a new family.

Other things about wedding parties also are changing. The custom of a mother and father jointly giving away their daughter is occurring in more than Jewish ceremonies. In some cases, the bride and groom walk down the aisle together, unaccompanied by parents. In others the bride and groom include their own vows and expressions of love and recognize other significant persons in the audience, such as grandparents, before the ceremony ends with readings or remarks. The point is that you should not assume that tradition rigidly prescribes a single kind of bridal party and that you should at least consider additional ways to involve family and close friends in the wedding ceremony.

3. **FINDING THE DRESS.** Whether they love classic elegance, daring creations or minimalist lines, all brides want their wedding gown to be the most beautiful ever, to see themselves in the mirror as they imagined they would look, probably long before they met their intended. Shopping for that dream dress can be a memorable adventure in itself.

You should not begin, however, until you have fixed the season, time of day and setting for your wedding. The reasons are obvious. A daytime wedding in your backyard will call for a very different dress from one for an evening affair in a palatial ballroom, determining, for just one example, whether or not you will wear a train. Once those decisions are made, you can take many routes to finding your perfect dress, beyond flipping through magazines and scrolling web sites. For example:

◆ **LOCAL SHOPS.** A number of Washington-area stores offer excellent wedding gown selections. They range from specialty shops to designer boutiques and include, among others, Rizik's, Saks Jandel, David's, Vera Wang and Priscilla of Boston. They stock from 25 to hundreds of dresses costing anywhere from bargain-basement sums to five figures. Some of the salons will personalize your dress. Theresa Sadd of Rizik's, for example, recalls a bride who wanted her deceased mother's pendent sewn into the hem. You also can have beading, lace or other trim from a loved one's wedding dress incorporated into your dress, your name embroidered on it, or other personal touches.

◆ **BRIDAL SHOWS.** Bridal shows are another good gown source. Held twice a year, in late summer and early winter, they are not only an excellent way to screen many service providers at once, but they usually have fashion shows that include the latest in bridal wear. Although they can be overcrowded at times, they are a good way to get a feel for what's out there and are

well worth attending. (Some specialty shops also have periodic fashion shows. Allegra's in Occoquan, Virginia, for instance, has one every spring and fall.)

◆ **HOMEMADE ELEGANCE.** If you're among the truly lucky, your dream dress will be made by your mother or a very close friend. One of my daughters-in-law was fortunate enough to have her mother design and make her gown. Not only was the style exactly what she wanted, but her mother was experienced enough to select the perfect fabric for an exceptionally elegant dress. Such luck results not only in the least costly dress you can acquire but also in one with added significance.

◆ **YOUR MOTHER'S OR GRANDMOTHER'S DRESS.** If it would mean a great deal to you to wear your mother's or grandmother's wedding dress, you should not rule that out just because it doesn't fit or it needs restoring. You can have it altered

Explaining the Ceremony

Religious and ethnic wedding ceremonies can be confusing or lack meaning if guests are unfamiliar with the customs involved. Couples need to make sure that the customs are explained to them.

If special attire is to be worn or certain items removed—shoes, for instance—before entering the ceremony site, guests should be told in advance, preferably through an insert card enclosed with the invitation.

At the ceremony itself, a program should be prepared and distributed to explain what is happening. At a Jewish wedding, for example,

it would explain that the canopy, or *chupah*, under which the vows are exchanged represents the new home, that seven blessings, or the *shevah brachot*, are sung, or that the groom steps on and breaks a glass at the end of the ceremony as a reminder of the destruction of the temple in Jerusalem.

It is also nice to introduce the wedding party in written form so guests have some knowledge of who's who. At one wedding I attended, the program also included those close to the couple who could not attend, and they were also referred to during the ceremony.

and its luster restored if it has faded. Steven Saidman of Imperial Gown Restoration and Preservation in Fairfax, Virginia, for example, says that much of his business today involves remodeling as well as restoring heirloom gowns. Similarly, DuPont Circle's Toast and Strawberries, owned by Rosemary Reed—author of *The Threads of Time*, a book on African-American designers and dressmakers since the 1850s—alters wedding gowns along with other apparel.

◆ **DESIGNER TRUNK SHOWS.** Designer trunk shows are another good gown source, and some salons will give a discount if a dress is purchased at a trunk show. Better yet, you get to talk to the designer and get his or her advice on what works best for you. You can check with your favorite shops or designer web sites, or watch for ads in *The Washington Post*, for trunk show schedules.

◆ **OFF TO KLEINFELD.** Some Washingtonians have been known to travel to Kleinfeld, the famous Brooklyn, New York, bridal salon, especially when it has its sample sales in January, February and October. The trip can turn into a lovely weekend experience for brides-to-be and their mothers or best friends. Here as elsewhere, however, beware of wanting to try on dress after dress. That can result in confusion and frustration, especially since Kleinfeld, which claims to sell "more wedding gowns than any other bridal salon on earth," offers over 10,000 designs.

◆ **CUSTOM-DESIGNED DRESSES.** If you don't find an existing dress that you can fall in love with, some shops will customize a dress for you or design and make one from scratch. Susan Ettenson of Allegra's, for example, says, "You name it, we can produce it." Alex Garcia of Foggy Bottom's Alex: Designer/Consigner and Toast and Strawberries are among others who

The Value of a Receiving Line

A receiving line is often considered old-fashioned and stuffy. But it does have its purpose.

Too often, the bride and groom don't greet guests personally. Instead, at the reception, they concentrate on each other or a few close friends. If you don't want to spend time on your special day visiting with guests during the reception, a receiving line following the ceremony works well. Realizing there are others behind them, guests tend to move along more quickly than if they encounter you at the reception, and you have at least had a few words with everyone.

Be careful, though, about those who seek you out at the reception. Have a plan to gracefully disengage yourself from lengthy conversations, and be sure to pay special attention to out-of-town guests. They have made a very special effort to join you. Don't ignore their presence.

Don't isolate yourself, either. Sweetheart tables (where only the bride and groom are seated at the reception) are romantic, but you do have an obligation to interact with your guests. Sweetheart tables can be a great refuge and a place to share a special moment, but spending most of your time there is discourteous.

will design original wedding gowns (as well as much else) for you.

◆ **RENTALS AND CONSIGNMENT SHOPS.** You can rent a wedding dress, but only the most frugal will be happy with that option. There is an emotional attachment to a wedding dress, which is why most of us couldn't bear to part with ours, why we have them specially cleaned and preserved regardless of whether they'll ever be worn again. Before deciding to rent, check out some consignment shops.

In the course of acquiring your dress, you should keep several things in mind:

◆ **A TRUSTED ADVISER.** Be sure to take your mother or a really good friend with you. You will need someone you can trust to tell you honestly how a dress looks.

◆ **CHANGING FASHIONS.** Bridal fashions change as quickly as the haute couture paraded annually on runways, so beware of being swayed by what's hot at the moment. That style could be on the "what's out" list by the time of your wedding.

◆ **ALTERATION POLICIES.** Before purchasing any dress, check the shop's alteration policy—some provide whatever alterations you wish, while others limit what they will do—and be sure to check alteration prices. At some stores, all but the slightest changes can add significantly to the cost of the dress.

◆ **COMFORT COUNTS.** Don't forget that the dress should be comfortable. You will wear it all day or evening. You will sit in it, walk in it, kneel in it, dance in it, eat in it and even visit the ladies' room in it. Wearing the dress also shouldn't cause beads of perspiration on your brow or blue lips and goose bumps on your shoulders.

◆ **APPOINTMENTS PREFERRED.** Most stores prefer that you make an appointment to view their collections, but some will accept walk-ins. Weekday appointments usually are available on short notice, but if you want to shop on a Saturday you should call at least a week in advance.

◆ **TOTAL-LOOK FITTINGS.** At your first fitting, usually about six weeks before the wedding, be sure to take your accessories, including undergarments and any jewelry you plan to wear. This is the time to preview your total look. At the second and final fitting, two to three weeks before the wedding, it's a good idea to have your hair and makeup done as well, so you will know exactly how you will look at your wedding.

Finally, a few modest points about others' attire:

◆ **THE GROOM: AVOIDING DISASTER.** Whether the groom plans to wear a tuxedo with a vest or cummerbund, white tie and tails, a white dinner jacket for an outdoor affair in summer or something else, he would be wise to pick up or try on his outfit a few days before the wedding. That way he can avoid the kind of disaster that befell one of my sons. This particular son put together a very special look for his wedding, taking pains to select the perfect tuxedo and accessories. On the morning of the big day, however, his designer duds were nowhere to be found—and the rental shop told him that there was nothing it could do. He had to settle for a patched-together, standard tuxedo and was deeply disappointed, to say the least. Many shops encourage early try-ons. If they don't, be sure to make arrangements to ensure you get what you ordered and that it fits well.

◆ **ATTENDANT DRESSES: NOT TOO MUCH DEMOCRACY.** Some have encouraged brides to pick a color and then simply ask her attendants to buy a dress they like in that color. No matter how much you love and respect those in your wedding party, however, can you really say that you love everything they wear? The only thing worse than one inappropriate attendant's dress is a variety of them, even if they are in the same color.

Granted, you are asking friends to make an

investment. Why not let them pick something they like and would wear again? Because this is your wedding, and you don't have to be that democratic. So long as you don't behave like a drill sergeant, you can solve any problem diplomatically and keep your attendants happy.

Once you have assembled your wedding party, invite the women (including the person who will pay for the flower girl's dress) for dinner on you at a favorite restaurant or at your home. This will be a relaxed time to reach consensus and determine a mutually acceptable style of dress and accessories as well as the costs involved. Obviously, any suggestions and preferences of style and color you have should be presented and discussed, but the more opportunity you can create for input from your attendants about what they will wear and pay will be greatly appreciated and significantly reduce the chances of later grumbling or hurt feelings.

◆ **MOTHERS' DRESSES: COORDINATION HELPS.** It's generally a good idea for the mothers of the couple to decide what colors each will wear and to discuss the style dress each prefers, so that they complement each other and don't clash—or, heaven forbid, show up in the same dresses.

After dealing with attire, you should get going on other plans, from scouting out wedding rings to booking musicians and photographers to deciding on a honeymoon spot. Make sure to pick a place with great appeal to both of you. You don't want to begin your marriage with one spouse sulking because he or she prefers lazing on a beach to trekking through the Himalayas. Whatever your choice, though, make reservations as soon as possible, lest your enchanted getaway gets sold out.

This would be a good time to take a break to enjoy each other and dream about your special day. There's still much to be done, but some things— such as choosing the menu, selecting flowers, picking linens and china, if applicable—are best left until a few months before the wedding. Caterers

and hotels change menus seasonally, and there's always something new in event planning. In such areas, you will be best off waiting to be sure you can take advantage of the latest that providers have to offer.

If you just can't stand being idle for the next couple of months and would feel better with a dress rehearsal, you can practice by planning an engagement party. That will give you a good feel for what's ahead, even if you're planning a formal wedding and decide on a casual engagement party.

GUEST LIST CHALLENGES

All the while, you will be doing much work on the guest list. This is not only because of the need for couples and parents and grandparents to collect many names and addresses and phone numbers (unfortunately, you may have to call some unresponsive guests to give the caterer an accurate count). It is also because the guest list is often one of the most contentious issues. It is not unusual for difficulties to arise between the two sets of parents, particularly the mothers, as well as between the couples and their parents or grandparents.

Sometimes the number of guests will be limited by venue capacity, other times by choice. Some couples simply don't want a "big fat (insert ethnicity) wedding," preferring instead an intimate gathering of immediate family and very close friends. Should that be your preference, you should indicate it when you announce your engagement. That will alert friends and subtly give notice to some not to expect an invitation.

Most guest list problems, however, stem, on the one hand, from budget limitations and on the other, from pressures to invite small armies. This may be because you and/or your betrothed have unusually large families (possibly expanded further by divorced parents). It may be because bride, groom and both sets of parents or grandparents all have large numbers of friends and associates. It may simply be because of a desire by the couple or the parents to share the day with everyone they know. But that usually isn't possible, so choices have to be made and/or adroit diplomacy employed.

At lunch recently, for example, I couldn't help overhearing the following conversation between a prospective bride and her mother:

DAUGHTER: *Would you like to start with the guest list?*

MOTHER: *No, let's order first.*

D: *All right. Would you like a glass of wine?*

M: *Yes, that would be nice.*

(Order arrives.)

D: *Okay, here's the list I've come up with.*

M: *Why is so-and-so being invited? I don't know her.*

D: *Okay, take her off.*

So it went until the 100-guest list had been pruned to 93, and the daughter congratulated her mother on how well they had done. With that, however, the mother asked to see the deleted names again. Only then did the daughter explain why they had been on the list: She had been to their weddings and felt that not inviting them would cause bad feelings with people she socializes with on a regular basis.

M: *Okay, put them back.*

D: *Thanks, mom. Would you like another glass of wine?*

That exchange contained a valuable lesson. Instead of making accusations or demands, the daughter took the time to listen to her mother's objections and complimented her. Only then did she explain about the deleted guests and give her mother time to rethink her decisions. More flies are caught with honey than with vinegar, every time.

Usually, though, guest list negotiations don't go that smoothly. More often than not, some people must be eliminated, and the problem generally can't be solved with the notion that seems to pop into everyone's mind: Invite some guests to the ceremony but not to the reception. In fact, that step can backfire, as the practice often is considered as much of a slight as not being invited at all. It is not easy for anybody to eliminate guests, but if enough are not cut to stay within budget, you either have to spend more or reduce the cost and quality of other parts of the wedding. Those usually are your choices.

At the outset, therefore, you would be wise to have everyone assign priorities to the guest list suggestions they make—at a minimum, those who "must" be invited and those who "should" be invited if possible. That will force you, as well as parents or grandparents, to be prepared for this issue from the start and provide much time for all to ponder the choices. There should then be no surprises if and when cuts must be made.

REMEMBERING WHOSE WEDDING IT IS

My dictionary defines a wedding first as "The act of marrying" and then as a "ceremony or celebration of a marriage." The act of marrying and the accompanying ceremony and celebration are centrally about the bride and groom, about their love, their fateful decision, their lifelong commitment. In short, the wedding is theirs, no matter how important it also may be to their families and friends. In all of the planning, it is valuable for everyone, and especially the parents, to keep this in mind, just as it is important for the couple to keep the sensitivities of their families and friends in mind.

There are, of course, still instances when parents, particularly the mothers of brides, are determined to dominate wedding plans, though this is less and less the case today. In part, that is because many couples are older when they marry and thus are more independent in their finances and in their thinking about what they want their wedding to be like. Even when parents are paying most or all of the bills, however, couples today often plan their wedding day the way they envision it, not the way Miss Manners or others might dictate. Departing from some traditions does not mean casting aside all etiquette—nothing can replace social grace and common courtesy—only injecting one's personal preferences and style in various ways.

When parents do pay the bills, it certainly is understandable for them to set financial guidelines for the couple, and the couple should be prepared to honor them. The bride especially, if her parents are paying for her clothes and the reception, must respect her parents' limitations. A bride can look stunning, after all, in a gown that costs less than the $5,000 number she thinks she can't live without.

Parents need to respect their children as well. If the couple has taken responsibility for the bills, parents need to heed their wishes. If they are asked to keep their guest list to a certain number, they certainly should do it. If parents feel strongly about inviting more guests than their allotment, they can offer to pay for the additional ones themselves. Similarly, if the bride and groom feel strongly about holding the wedding in a certain place, parents ultimately should agree to their wishes, even if the parents fear that some family members or friends might have difficulty attending. Prolonged arguments over such matters are not worth the price of ruining your child's wedding plans, let alone of jeopardizing the deep love between parent and child.

When there are serious disagreements, it can of course be painful for both parties. It is not unheard of, for example, for parents to be displeased by those their children choose to marry. It is perfectly acceptable, I think, for a parent to make this known early on to his or her child, to make the case for parental opposition openly but calmly. It is acceptable, at least, to do so one time—and then to listen carefully to the child and, in the end, to respect his or her decision. Yes, this is much easier said than done. Such conflicts, after all, are the stuff of human tragedy, especially when children choose spouses of a different race, religion or ethnic background. In Romeo and Juliet, one does not expect the Capulets and the Montagues to say, "Hey, it's the kids' decision." If the marriage proceeds, however, I would urge the parents to put the child's wishes before their own, to try to be civil, even gracious, about the union, as difficult as that might be. Otherwise, I believe, there are likely to be even more painful consequences ahead for all involved.

To me, any parent acting badly about a child's wedding is unacceptable. If divorced parents do so, it is doubly unacceptable. No matter what has happened between divorced couples, they should remember that a wedding is a time for love to prevail, for the bride to enjoy the day of her dreams, not for divorced parents to engage in acts of revenge. The point is that for all parents, a child's wedding day is not a time for parents to think mainly of themselves. The bride and groom should, of course, be as sensitive and respectful as possible about the wishes of their parents and grandparents, doing whatever they can to accommodate them. When all is said and done, though, it is the wishes of the bride and groom that should be uppermost in everyone's mind. ◆

CHAPTER XV

Giving and Getting Gifts and Favors

A gift consists not in what is done or given,
but in the intention of the giver or doer.

—LUCIUS ANNAEUS SENECA

IT REALLY IS BETTER to give than to receive, especially if the gesture is made in the true spirit of the act. But being on the receiving end isn't so bad, either. So if everyone loves gifts, whether given or received, why are so many people so uncomfortable with gift-giving questions? Many hosts and hostesses worry about how to tell those they invite to a housewarming, a birthday or a retirement party, for instance, not to bring gifts, please. Some wedding couples cringe over registry lists, and some guests wring their hands over the right thing to do.

Well, do as you like—so long as you like what you do and you keep certain basics in mind. For example, bridal registries are one thing; young couples just starting out need certain things. As a rule, however, gifts should be festive rather than utilitarian. I'm especially against giving practical items that recipients are likely to buy for themselves anyway. This is not to say that you shouldn't buy a unique gift that reflects a friend's style. That's the idea. But this doesn't mean that you should buy a television for a woman friend who may want one (unless she is lost without one and you know that she can't afford it). Stick to something that will surprise and delight her, and that includes such gifts as striking crystal and porcelain creations, sculptures, antiques and other creative items, even if many might gather dust on a shelf for years. As Picasso said, "Art washes away from the soul the dust of everyday life." The right "dust collector" gifts can brighten the soul in this way as well. So give a gift from the heart, and watch a spirit soar. *(See p. 82 for other ideas.)*

Another thing to remember is that gifts are customary, not obligatory. Hopefully, you will be invited to an anniversary affair or graduation party or other celebration chiefly because the host or hostess wants you to share in the joy of the occasion, not because they expect a gift. Hopefully, wedding couples you know (and their parents) are not among those who feel that since they are spending a tidy sum to include you in their joyous day, they are entitled to a fairly expensive present. Hopefully, you won't be told that, "In lieu of gifts please make a donation to our political candidate's campaign… to our honeymoon … to our house down payment."

The do-unto-others lesson of all this is to avoid entitlement attitudes about gifts when you are throwing the party. This goes for asking, on invitations, that no gifts be brought. No matter how well intentioned the thought may be, you should avoid doing it, for two reasons. On the one hand, while guests are not obliged to bring a gift to begin with, including the "no gifts, please" statement makes the opposite assumption. On the other hand, you run the risk of appearing cheeky for declining a gesture of kindness. If you do prefer no presents, it is wiser to get the word out through family and friends that gifts are not necessary.

With weddings, though, you are expected to give gifts to the attendants, this time with good reason. After asking attendants to invest a fair amount of time and money on their nuptials, the wedding couple should show their appreciation with a gift, one within their means, and the choices are many. Jewelry has always been popular, but many bridal attendants secretly admit that such baubles generally find a permanent home in a jewelry box. Some

recommend gifts geared toward the attendants' personal interests, though a subscription to *Popular Mechanics* or *Cooking Light* is not what they have in mind. An antique silver box for your friend who spends every spare moment "junquing" would be a much better choice. So would hand-painted Italian pottery for a friend who is still looking for her place under the Tuscan sun, or a gift certificate to the Ritz Carlton or Four Seasons hotel chains for friends with wanderlust.

Good selections are available at area department stores, where many of the buyers have a knack for innovative, one-off pieces to delight the most discriminating friend. Quality gift shops also abound in the Washington area. An unusual "just for you" gift can be had, for example, at Arts Afire Glass Gallery in Old Town, Alexandria, Virginia, which has the

---

Some Don'ts and Do's About Gifts

When it comes to gift giving or receiving, you would do well to remember the following:

DON'TS

◆ Don't include gift information of any sort on an invitation.

◆ Don't ask guests to support you financially in any way.

◆ For weddings, don't register for outlandishly expensive gifts. Your registry should be in line with the financial means of your guests.

DO'S

◆ Do register in stores and on-line for wedding gifts, including for more than first-time marriages.

◆ Do get the word out through family and friends where you are registered.

◆ Whatever the occasion, if you prefer that there be no presents, do get the word out through family and friends that gifts are not necessary.

◆ Do accept any gift with sincere thanks—and with a thank you note.

◆ Do ask guests to support a charitable cause.

largest collection of kaleidoscopes in the metropolitan area. The gallery can arrange to customize almost any kaleidoscope to match the interests of those in your party. Owner Joe Egerton says that special kaleidoscopes have been made, for example, for vinophiles or fishermen, and brides and grooms even can give each other kaleidoscopes with details about themselves and/or their weddings incorporated into the scope patterns.

As for favors, a trend is emerging, and a rather good one, I think, for people to turn favors into charitable donations. Not long ago, for example, a *Parade* magazine article told of a couple who, on their wedding day, took guests on a shopping expedition to a toy store, each armed with a $15 cash favor, to buy goodies for the annual Toys for Tots Marine Corps Reserve program. Their presence certainly was noticed (not many brides and grooms show up at toy stores on a Saturday afternoon), and many regular customers bought toys to contribute to the effort. Adding to the excitement, most guests spent a good deal more than their allotted funds, enabling several trucks to be filled with toys for distribution.

Of course, regular favors come in many forms, from heart-shaped anything on Valentine's Day to a pretty box of shamrocks for good luck on St. Patrick's Day to wedding candies or even beach flip-flops with your initials embossed on the soles, the better to leave your footprints in the sand. (Mark Solomon of IDPartnersonline, a novelty company that provides favors, says that the flip-flops are popular with destination-wedding couples tying the knot on a beach.) One of the most impressive wedding touches I've heard about, however, was simply a note from the couple perched atop each guest's place setting. Each note was handwritten, personalized and expressed the couple's delight in the guest's presence. Time-consuming? Yes. Appreciated? You bet. While such a gesture probably can only be done at affairs with a limited number of guests, it is one more example of the fact that good taste is not necessarily expensive. ◆

CHAPTER XVI

The Dotted Lines

Some Thoughts on Contracts and Insurance

WHAT IS THE CHANCE of something going wrong with the photography at your celebration? Not very high, right? Well, yes . . . but it can happen. Indeed, it has happened. A magazine photojournalist I worked with, for example, shot a major Washington event only to discover that his film hadn't transported. Luckily, his picture could be re-shot and no harm was done. But there would be no happy ending if photos of your affair were to turn out blank.

Similar questions could be asked about many aspects of a celebration. What if a guest is hurt on the premises? What if the flowers wilt? What if a seamstress fails to deliver a promised wedding dress? All are unlikely . . . but they can happen. Remember, after all, the caterer who failed to show up for the wedding of one couple. *(See p. 36.)*

You cannot, of course, be expected to foresee and forestall all potential mishaps. Among the things you can do, however, is make sure that all vendor contracts provide you with reasonable protection and that you also are covered by insurance.

CONTRACTS

Most people will not want to add a "lawyer's fees" line to their budgets. But if you have an exceptionally low tolerance for risk, if you plan to spend out-sized sums (say $100,000 or more) or if you have

any concerns at all, it might be wise to consult an attorney.

I am not a lawyer. The following suggestions are based on common sense and years of dealing with vendors for an array of events. They are offered for your consideration before you decide whether or not to seek legal advice.

◆ **LIABILITY ISSUES.** Be sure to read carefully any contract section on liability issues, and pay special attention to any wording about damage and injury. For example, if a contract says that the vendor will not be responsible for more than $250 in damages and far more money is involved, you should discuss renegotiating that provision.

◆ **WHAT MATTERS MOST TO YOU.** Most people care more about one aspect of an affair over everything else. If you are slightly obsessed about the flowers, for instance, pay particular attention to that vendor and the contract you sign. Should something go wrong in this area, your reaction is likely to be more severe than if a problem pops up with an element that doesn't mean as much to you. You are best protected if the contract spells out exactly what the vendor is obligated to provide. In the case of flowers, for example, make sure that the contract describes precisely how you want the bridal bouquet, the centerpieces, etc. to look. Consider attaching a photograph to the contract of individual arrangements that you have selected.

◆ **SUBSTITUTE PROVIDERS.** Be sure that the vendor cannot have someone else perform the designated services without your permission. Usually, the vendor's right to assign the work to someone else is set forth in the contract. Make sure that the contract gives you the final say before the vendor can have a substitute do the work.

◆ **ASKING QUESTIONS.** Read the fine print of any contract or policy, ask for clarification of anything you don't understand, and don't sign anything until you feel comfortable and completely understand the contents.

◆ **KEEPING YOUR OPTIONS OPEN.** Make sure that you understand whether you can get out of the contract if you need to, and the consequences of doing so.

◆ **ORAL CONTRACTS.** Yes, oral contracts are binding, but they are difficult to enforce. That may be why Samuel Goldwyn is alleged to have said, "A verbal contract isn't worth the paper it is written on." A signed contract obviously provides more protection. To be sure, dealing with contracts can be tedious, but whatever it takes to negotiate a document you're comfortable with will be well worth the effort should you need to fall back on the terms of your contract.

INSURANCE

Regarding insurance, you should keep several things in mind:

◆ **SPECIAL EVENT POLICY.** If you wish, you can buy a special event policy. Fireman's Fund, for example, offers wedding insurance and will cover stolen gifts from your reception site, damage to your wedding dress, defective film or cancellation of the event for reasons beyond your control. However, many companies won't provide coverage or will restrict coverage if alcohol is to be served. In general, coverage in such policies is limited to certain terms and conditions, so be sure to make a list of your particular concerns before contacting any insurance company.

◆ **HOMEOWNER RIDER.** My-son-the-insurance-agent notes, "You can also add a rider to your homeowner's policy to cover you in such instances, whether the event is held at your home or not." If you decide to acquire any kind of additional coverage, contact your agent at least a month in advance.

◆ **VENDOR INSURANCE.** Make sure that any firm you contract with is properly covered.

◆ **BECOMING AN "ADDITIONAL INSURED."** In the event of injury or damage, most venues, houses of worship, transportation companies and other service providers have insurance policies to which you can be named as an "additional insured." Inquire about this possibility and ask to be included in the policies.

◆ **ADEQUATE PROTECTION.** Be sure that the insurance is adequate in the unlikely event that someone is injured at your event or if the venue or vehicle you rent is damaged.

It is, of course, no fun to think of what could go wrong at your event. It is even less fun, though, if you have no protection against mishaps. So pay some heed to these matters. ◆

CHAPTER XVII

Picks of Some Pros...

TO HELP GET YOU STARTED on the road to a successful celebration, we surveyed professionals in the Washington region about which vendors and venues they consider the area's best. More than 60 professionals responded, providing their top three choices in each category. Following is a weighted ranking of their picks:[1]

CAKES
1. Patty Cakes
2. Creative Cakes
3. Andrea Webster Cake[2]

CATERERS
1. Occasions
2. Design Cuisine
3. Ridgewells

ENTERTAINMENT
1. Cast of Thousands
2. Washington Talent Agency
3. Peanut Butter[3]

FLORISTS
1. Amaryllis
2. Foxglove
3. Exquisite Floral Design

INVITATIONS
1. Creative Parties
2. Wrap It Up
3. The Written Word

MUSIC
1. Bialek's Music
2. Washington Talent Agency
3. Entertainment Exchange

PHOTOGRAPHERS
1. Neal Freed
2. Clay Blackmore
3. Photographer's Gallery

PLANNERS 1
Weddings
1. Bonnie Schwartz
2. Creative Parties
3. Engaging Affairs

PLANNERS 2
Events
1. Creative Parties
2. Jodi Moraru*
2. Rave Reviews*
Numbers 2 and 3 were tied.

RENTAL COMPANIES 1
China, Linen & Silverware
1. Perfect Settings
2. DC Rentals
3. Party Rentals

RENTAL COMPANIES 2
Tents, Tables & Chairs
1. HDO Rentals
2. Classic Tents
3. Sugar Plum Tents

TRANSPORTATION
1. Atlantic Valet
2. Regal Limo
3. Carey Worldwide

VENUES I
Historic & Museums
1. National Museum of Women in the Arts
2. Corcoran
3. Building Museum

VENUES 2
Mansions & Manors
1. Meridian House
2. Dumbarton House
3. Oxon Hill Manor

VENUES 3
Country Inns
1. Inn at Little Washington
2. Keswick Hall
3. Morrison House

VENUES 4
Other Popular Sites
1. Ronald Reagan Building
2. The Gallerie at Lafayette Center
3. Union Station

VIDEOGRAPHERS
1. Online Suburban Video
2. Jenny Lehman
3. Thomas Bowen

[1] *This survey is not intended to be a scientific representation of every event professional in the region, only the weighted ranking of more than 60 pros' picks. Each of their first-place votes was given a weight of 3 points, second place mentions 2 points and third place choices 1 point. The results were ranked according to those receiving the highest, second highest and third highest number of points in each category.*

[2] *This provider no longer works in the Washington area.*

[3] *It could not be confirmed that this provider services the Washington area.*

CHAPTER XVIII

...And Other Good Advice

TO PROVIDE STILL MORE perspectives, I asked an additional eight colleagues with wide experience in planning events—from modest dinner parties to gatherings of hundreds for fundraisers or corporate affairs—to provide their wisdom. They offered some unique notions on such things as ways to save money and the "Cinderella complex"— the desire of Washingtonians to get home before midnight, which requires events to be scripted to end by 10 p.m. Here is their advice on an array of matters:

A Successful Party Recipe

NANCY CHISTOLINI

INGREDIENTS
Theme
Location
Guest List
Invitations
Menu
Favors
Personal Touches

All parties require a theme, whether for a birthday, anniversary, promotion, retirement or corporate event. Add the location, the guest list, the invitation, the food and the favors. Combine with the most important ingredient—the personal touch— and follow directions.

PREPARE THE INVITATION.
The invitation should tell the guests what to expect. Formal or informal? Gift or no gift? Directions? RSVP by? Give all necessary details.

BLEND THE GUESTS.
Get the guests attention as soon as they enter. Be at the door to welcome them. Consider an icebreaker

to get the party started. For example, at a Christmas party, give each guest a pair of antlers. It gets the conversation going immediately.

GRADUALLY ADD FOOD AND DRINK.
Entertaining should be warm and gracious, whether for a small family gathering or a large corporate event. Select a caterer that can provide everything—tablecloths, china, stemware and staff. The food can be as elegant as the occasion, but I always like to add one appetizer or entrée that is a crowd-pleaser. That means something that everyone knows and doesn't have to ask the wait staff, "What is that?"

STIR IN SOME MEMORIES.
Have someone take Polaroid photos and put them near the door, so guests have souvenirs.

Here are a couple of ways that I have added extra touches to the recipe:

A TEA PARTY.

I hosted a tea for a woman who volunteered for many causes. She was glamorous and always dressed to the nines, with a hat and wonderful jewelry. For personal touches I put hats on head forms down the middle of the stairs in the center hallway. As soon as guests arrived, they saw the hats. Instead of flowers on the café tables, I used lots of strands of pearls and pins. The cake was made in the shape of a wide-brimmed hat. When each guest left, they were given a favor bag. It was a white bag folded to look like a tea bag, complete with a string attached to a tag. On each tag I wrote a special message about the guest of honor.

A PROMOTION PARTY.

An executive received a promotion and was honored at a cocktail party. He was fastidious about his appearance and always had the latest eyeglass frames. At the time, the style was a heavy black frame. When guests arrived, each was secretly given a pair of the look-alike frames. When the honoree went to the podium to make remarks, the entire audience put on the glasses. He turned around and saw 100 people in his eyeglasses.

I also have a few rules for keeping down recipe costs:

1. If using a caterer, give an accurate count. Do not give 10 over or 10 under. There will always be someone who has to cancel at the last minute, but the "head count" translates into dollars.

2. Serve only wine, sparkling water and soda—it is not always necessary to have a complete bar. It is also interesting to serve Marguerita's or Piña Colada's for a summer party, instead of wine.

3. Plan a menu with variety, including variety of color, and moderate portions. I once attended a dinner party where everything served was white…on white china. And moderate portions are best: Guests are coming for dinner, not going to the crusades. ◆

Nancy Chistolini is Senior Vice President, Fashion and Public Relations, at Hecht's.

Details, Details, Details

JENNIFER COVER PAYNE

PLANNING, detailed timelines and targeted goals help make events successful. Figure out every detail of the event from the time the guests drive up until the time they leave. Do a dress rehearsal. Visit the event venue at least three times to be sure that all possible details are covered. Knowing where guests can park, for example, is important. When doing events in an area where there is limited parking, it makes sense to provide valet parking. It can take an hour to calm down a frustrated guest who couldn't find parking.

Guests have to feel that they are valued and welcomed. They should be greeted when they arrive and should not have to wait more than two minutes for seat assignments. The reception is prelude to the event. For events with 400 or fewer guests, seat assignments can be in alpha order on placards on a table, at least if there are volunteers to assist guests in locating their names. If there are more than 400 guests, use file boxes, manned by volunteers, with guest names on cards in alpha order.

Once guests are through the check-in, provide food and drink. If dinner won't be served for more than an hour from the start time of the event, offer appetizers with cocktails. As for background music, which creates atmosphere, the musicians should be accustomed to playing for crowds that don't focus on them. Once the room is full, the bodies in the room will absorb the music. The music should never drown out the talking. When guests have to raise their voices to be heard, the music is too loud. Music during dinner needs to be soft, or else there should be none.

THE VENUE: CHARACTER AND CONVENIENCE. Where the event is held is exceedingly important. The venue should have character and charm. If the venue is a hotel, the selection of linens, flowers and lighting become key to creating atmosphere. Historic sites are great for events, but they often present challenges that hotels do not. Hotels have unlimited staff to assist in setting up and to accommodate last-minute changes, at least reasonable ones. In many historic sites, you must make all arrangements for event set-up in advance, and last-minute needs cannot be met.

Have volunteers with table charts to help guests find their seats, and clearly number every table. Be sure that the room has enough light for guests to find their table and each other.

Food can make or break an event. I have never heard anyone speak highly of an event that had bad wine or food. Even if the event is held in a palace, if the food or wine is bad, that becomes part of the event legacy until the next year. I have heard rave reviews about bountiful and delicious feasts served in average places. Food can bond strangers together. Of course, there has to be a reason for the coming together, and a program that moves quickly and provides some inspiration is a key component to a good evening.

The program is always a challenge. People from the Washington area believe that if the event lasts beyond 10 p.m., it is too long. It doesn't matter whether it is on a weekday or a weekend—they all seem to have a Cinderella complex: They have to be home before midnight. You can control the program by scripting everyone you can script and giving time limits to the honorees. Then take a deep breath when the grateful honorees exceed their three minutes. Assume that they will go over time—and plan for that detail as well.

Jennifer Cover Payne is Executive Director of the Cultural Alliance of Greater Washington

Reality Entertaining at Home

COLLEEN EVANS

HERE ARE FOUR thoughts on entertaining at home, and on a relatively modest budget:

1. **THE GROUP.** I always invite an eclectic group— some from work or the media, some old friends, neighbors I like, and some friends who are very friendly, a little "over the top," to put everyone at ease (these types also can act as the entertainment).

2. **THE CHOW.** I prefer easy food (either made ahead or brought in from Whole Foods or fast food), so I can circulate and enjoy my party. I've served everything from big pans of homemade lasagna to Popeyes fried chicken, my famous Tuna Noodle Casserole Good Friday dinner (Mac and cheese for the seafood challenged), Nic-o-Bolis overnighted from Nicola's in Rehoboth Beach, Delaware, and, of course, Costco!

I never have too many choices—but always enough of whatever I'm serving to feed an army buffet style and just enough choices to satisfy the meat eaters, vegetarians and people with a sweet tooth. I serve red/white wine, beer and one specialty theme drink that can be made ahead of time and served in big pitchers over ice (mojitos, white poinsettia's made with white cranberry juice and vodka, margaritas).

If more than 10 people are coming, it's paper plates/napkins (the good kind, like Chinette, not the cheap generic) and plastic cups (except for wine, for which I'll use my mismatched wineglasses) but real silverware.

3. **THE ATMOSPHERE.** I always keep the atmosphere very informal; my guests know that they are welcome to bring a friend.

4. THE HELP. Hire at least one or two people to help keep the place clean throughout the party—to pick up plates, napkins and cups, to put the food out/away, to empty ashtrays. Yes, I occasionally let people smoke in one designated room or outside on the patio. In my house the living room is smoking central; we plan on having it redone, so I don't care about the carpet or drapes getting smelly, and it's far enough away from the other rooms that no one is offended.

If you want to hire a few people to help with serving/clean-up, find friends in the hotel/restaurant business. They'll know people in banquets or the kitchen who are always looking to earn extra money and also know how to serve/clean up, along with how to display food. Your prospects of success increase substantially if it's a holiday, as some restaurants/hotels are very slow or closed on Thanksgiving, Christmas, Memorial Day, July Fourth, Labor Day, or the employees are from another country and don't celebrate U.S. holidays.

Colleen Evans is Public Relations Director of Ritz Carlton Hotels in Washington.

Price, Lemons and Tight Seating

RIMA CALDERON

A QUICK TAKE on planning events:

SAVING MONEY. It's very important to know how much you are prepared to spend and to communicate that information to the caterer, flower designer, etc. These companies want our business (and our return business), and they are happy to work with us on price, especially when we're clear about our budget. Also, although fresh flowers are lovely, they aren't always necessary. Flower designers have done colorful, informal centerpieces of lemons and limes or potted plants.

SUCCESS. Other than having fascinating people attend, I think an essential ingredient for success is creating an electric atmosphere. At a seated dinner, for example, small tables with as many people as possible at each table are much better than 6-foot rounds with lots of space between guests. Tight seating makes for much more conversation and fun. At receptions, well-defined spaces where people gather and feel a bit crowded is more entertaining than wide open spaces.

Rima Calderon is Director, Corporate Communications, The Washington Post Company.

Simplicity Saves

MARIANNE BECTON

ONE IMPORTANT thing to remember about planning events is that simplicity saves (and, conversely, complexity costs).

By simplicity I mean, above all, reducing the number of vendors and working with a venue's supplier team. You will reap savings not only in terms of money but also in terms of fewer slipups. This is because simplicity strengthens two critical elements: communication and coordination.

Reducing the number of vendors self-evidently reduces your reliance on cross-vendor communication. (Anyone who has tried to make sure that all vendors for an event regularly check with each other knows the problem.) Events also hinge on coordination, on all pieces working together at the right time. By reducing the number of vendors, you reduce the number of hand-offs, another blessing. So use a single vendor, and its supply chain, for as many elements as the vendor can provide.

You would also be wise to keep other elements of the event as simple as possible, including the invitations, the program and the menu.

There are other ways to save money as well. For example:

◆ **PLAN AHEAD.** Last-minute shopping costs you more.

◆ **PACKAGED SERVICES.** If the venue offers catering, photographer and flowers, you may save by using their suppliers.

◆ **USE CONTRACTS AND ADHERE TO THEM.** Include dates and penalty clauses when possible.

◆ **OVERESTIMATE RATHER THAN UNDERESTIMATE ATTENDANCE.** Adding more plates at the last minute, if it can be done, will cost more.

Finally, here are what I consider some essential ingredients for event planning:

◆ **SITE VISITS.** Be sure to visit the venue before you contract for an event.

◆ **EXPECTATIONS.** Make sure that stakeholders, vendors and guests all know what is expected of them.

◆ **QUALITY.** Focus on quality, not quantity. If you must choose between value and choices, take fewer menu choices in favor of better quality food, and make sure that parking arrangements are sufficient to include valet drop-off and pick-up.

Marianne Becton is Director, Strategic Alliances Group Public Policy and External Affairs, of Verizon.

Money Isn't Everything

LINDA ERDOS

AS SOMEONE WHO journeyed from private industry to the Arlington County Public Schools, I have learned that you can make good impressions at events without putting a huge dent in your budget.

Before I arrived, the usual plan for gatherings hosted by the school system called for using the schools' own food services. With a little creativity, however, I found that even within our limited budget we could hire an outside caterer, as well as rental firms, to put the school system's best foot forward at a reasonable price.

For example, by hiring a local caterer, we can provide an array of appetizers and finger foods, supplemented with a range of fresh fruits or confections from local wholesale outlets or discount suppliers.

The caterer delivers the food on disposable plastic trays, which we duly discard. Instead, we employ the school system's wide selection of silver, crystal and china serving pieces, augmented by serving pieces that staff members bring from home—and a wonderful transformation takes place. Add attractive table linens from the rental firm, along with some small cocktail tables, and the result is an event that people recognize as a special effort to make them feel special.

At a countywide event for school partners, business partners in the hotel or restaurant industry contribute a large portion of the food. The resulting savings enable us to hire tuxedoed wait staff to add an elegant touch to the occasion. Recognition is given to donors with tent cards at buffet tables and acknowledgements in the event program.

Using the school system's own music and arts groups, we provide entertainment for various events at little or no cost—which also provides a wonderful opportunity to showcase the diverse talents of our students.

By using the school system's own resources, and involving business partners in as many ways as possible, the opportunity to create special events for special occasions has been dramatically enhanced. The lesson is simple. A little thought and creativity can go a long way toward creating the impression you wish to convey—and you can do it at a reasonable cost.

Linda Erdos is Director of School and Community Relations, Arlington Public Schools.

Six Aspects Of Event Planning

ALICE CONWAY

YOU HAVE BEEN ASKED to plan an event, whether your employer's business anniversary or your child's wedding. You start to envision blue and silver lights, swatches of aqua and purple linens and lovely flowers, and you begin hearing strings or harps or perhaps a jazz trio. Then you have to snap out of it and get down to business.

At Stratford University, you would learn a great deal about the different phases of required work—research, design, planning, coordination and evaluation—but I will limit myself here to half a dozen basics:

1. **IDENTIFYING DIFFERING AGENDAS.** As part of your research, identify both the overt and covert purpose for the event.

   For example, the parents of the bride may sincerely want to give their daughter the wedding of her dreams. But they may also want the reception to impress their friends and business associates. You have to balance the wedding couple's objectives with those of the parents (a challenge many will find familiar).

   With a nonprofit group, budgets may suggest the need for a moderately priced annual fundraiser, so that net receipts meet the group's goal. But the executive director or board of directors (or their spouses) may want a more elaborate affair for business or personal reasons or to generate publicity.

   Such differing agendas can seriously challenge the success of an event. Thus you must research all the issues, identify the decisionmakers and constantly juggle the aims of different parties.

2. **MATTERS OF SCHEDULING.** In your planning, peak periods, traffic patterns and weather conditions should all be scrutinized before deciding on the date for your affair.

   Whatever the occasion, Saturday is the highest-demand day for events, especially during holidays. This means that venues are booked more than a year in advance, that Saturday prices are highest, and that even if you do get the venue you want that day, it may be hard for guests to come (there are sooooo many invitations). Availability thus is greater on Friday or Sunday, and your guest acceptances and prices will reflect this fact.

   If you expect a lot of out-of-towners to come, don't hold the event in February, when snow can play havoc with flying or driving. It is also wise to schedule an event to begin after rush hour traffic has subsided (well, do the best you can) so guests don't arrive late and stressed.

3. **QUESTIONS OF LOCATION.** A number of factors need to be considered about the event site. Among them:

   ◆ Think always of the comfort of your guests. Safety, parking, metro proximity, ADA access— all are critical factors when choosing a venue. (So are time of day, attire and natural light.)

   ◆ Accommodating all guests in one room, and one

with no obstructed views, is important for some events, particularly when there is a program and speakers.

♦ Be sure the venue can support all aspects of the events, from décor to guest arrival and flow to sufficient space for food preparation and service.

4. EVENT TIMING AND TEMPO. This encompasses several considerations as well:

♦ Be sure you have enough time to plan the event—or be prepared to make compromises.

♦ Create a timeline. It is the most important tool you can have. It should start from the moment an event is planned until the last bill is paid, the thank you notes are sent and the evaluation is complete. A comprehensive timeline will ensure that invitations get printed on time, that linens and the flowers are ordered and that all deliveries are on time.

♦ Tempo is the pace of the actual event. It needs to be orchestrated from start to finish: when vendors arrive, set-up time, guest arrival, the program (if any), when food is served, music played and speeches made. Set a realistic production schedule.

5. DOING A SWOT ANALYSIS. Pardon the professional parlance, but a SWOT analysis—a study of strengths, weaknesses, opportunities and threats—should be done, especially for (but not limited to) such events as corporate meetings, trade association gatherings or nonprofit fundraisers. The elements:

♦ Realistically evaluate the event's strengths in terms of budget, honoree, guests, volunteer support and location.

♦ Recognize an event's weaknesses. A SWOT analysis of a fundraising event, for example, might indicate inadequate manpower (paid or volunteer) or an insufficient donor base, early-warning signs that have to be addressed.

♦ Opportunities are the bonuses hoped for in every event. Be prepared for them. Have a press release available in the event of last-minute press coverage. Use of décor or flowers from a previous evening's event can save considerable cost, as can a performance or cameo appearance by a resident entertainer or one who is in town for another reason.

♦ Threats must be anticipated. Threats used to center mainly on the weather—snow and rain, flight delays, traffic jams and power outages. Now everyone must focus on threats with a new mindset: security and safety. Registration and food preparations, exit routes and access points must be secured and tested. Evacuation plans must be in place for the smallest gathering. Since this is new for Americans, experts should be consulted.

6. POST-EVENT EVALUATION. Post-event evaluations are not reserved for professionals. Knowing what went well and what didn't will be extremely helpful in planning your next celebration.

Alice Conway, CSEP, is the Director of the Event Management Program at Stratford University in Falls Church, Virginia.

One for the List People

LINDA LEVY GROSSMAN

I BELONG TO the worldwide population of List People. I routinely make lists of everything I have to do in life and look forward to checking off each task as it is completed. This gives me the sense (okay, sometimes the illusion) that I have things under control. I offer, therefore, a basic list of what needs to be done to plan a personal or professional event:

1. ORGANIZATION

- Determine what the event must accomplish.
- Develop budget.
- Design timetable.
- Delegate tasks.

2. ESTABLISH A BUDGET

- Understand your resources.
- Monitor all expenses.
- Modify budget for essential reasons only.
- Pursue value for your dollar.
- Broaden creativity when limited by budget.
- Borrow or barter whenever possible.

3. COMMUNICATION

- Don't allow too few to "own" too much.
- Provide all information to all involved.
- Keep information flowing.
- Never assume anything.

4. VENDOR MANAGEMENT

- Evaluate your time vs. vendor fees.
- Negotiate whenever possible.
- Understand all terms.
- Select vendors experienced for the task.
- Select vendors who share your vision.
- Form partnerships and establish relationships.

5. THEME AND DECOR

- Perception is everything.
- Don't let a theme become too self-serving.
- Don't try to be different for difference sake.

6. PLEASING YOUR GUESTS

- What do they want?
- What do they expect?
- Why are they coming?
- What is important to them?
- What is not important to them?

The answers to these questions are very different for a fundraising event, a corporate event or a social event. Take a look at the following box for the answers:

What do your guests care about	Nonprofit fundraising event	Corporate event	Social event
Accessibility to talk/ mingle/network	yes	yes	yes
Ambiance	yes	yes	yes
Bars; ease to get a drink	yes	yes	yes
Duration (shortness)	yes	yes	no
Food	yes	yes	yes
Gift bags	yes	yes	yes
Music	some do	no	yes
Organization	yes	yes	yes
Parking	yes	yes	yes
People to help and answer questions	yes	yes	yes
Perceived cost/ how the money is being used	yes	yes	no
Service	yes	yes	yes
Speeches	no	no	yes
Venue	yes	yes	yes

Linda Levy Grossman is Executive Director of The Helen Hayes Awards.

A Directory Of Service Providers

THE SERVICE PROVIDERS listed include firms with whom I have had personal experience and vendors who were recommended by professional colleagues or whose work I have observed at area bridal shows. To provide variety and choice, additional vendors were selected from various media, including the Internet, newspaper articles and ads or commercials.

While some of the finest professionals in the industry are listed here, only some providers noted in the editorial section of the book have been evaluated, not everyone included in this directory. Every attempt was made, however, to check each listing for accuracy.

Space limitations made it necessary to confine listings to name, phone number, web address and, where appropriate, capacity. Please note that the majority of vendors serve the entire metropolitan area. While listings have been grouped according to area jurisdictions—i.e., Maryland, Virginia and the District of Columbia—a caterer in Maryland, for instance, will serve your party in Virginia, and so on. (Some will even travel to other states or countries.) Venues, on the other hand, are generally chosen because of proximity to a ceremony site or other specific circumstances. Therefore, location has been included in the Venues section. *(To understand additional coded information, see the box on p. 111 for keys.)*

We hope that this directory will be of assistance in choosing the service providers best suited to help you orchestrate a successful celebration.

BRIDAL ATTIRE/FORMAL WEAR

Maryland

The Bridal Boutique – 410-290-5666

Bridal Images – 301-738-9080/ www.bridalimages.com

Bridal Visions – 301-568-6120

Bridals Direct – 301-350-6640

Carmen's Bridal Fashions – 301-445-7519/ www.carmensbridal.com

Claire Dratch – 301-656-8000

Country Miss Bridal – 301-627-2775/ www.cmbridal.com

David's Bridal – 301-881-1112/ www.davidsbridal.com

Discount Bridal Service – 301-670-0032

Distinctive Designs Bridal – 301-948-1833/ www.ddbridal.com

Francesca's – 410-882-5050

G Street Fabrics – 301-231-8998/ www.gstreetfabrics.com

Gamberdella Inc. – 410-828-7870

Grace & Elegance Bridal & Tuxedo Shop – 410-266-9490/www.bridalrental.com

Hats by Haber – 301-649-2676/www.hatalog.com

Helen's Bridal – 301-309-6868

I Do I Do Wedding Gowns – 301-762-4464/ www.idoidoweddinggowns.com

Joan Jenkins Bridal/Alterations – 301-695-9344

Kaufman's Wedding World – 301-695-7898/ www.weddingworld.com

Kelly's Kollection – 410-494-8890

Labella Bridal & Tuxedo Shop – 410-882-2888

Lefty's Bridal & Boutique, Inc. – 301-420-2922/
    www.leftysbridal.com

M'Jourdelle – 410-337-0490

Designs by Nicole – 301-570-4720

Niko's Bridal Fashions – 410-675-0081/
    www.nikobridal.com

Parkway Custom Drycleaning/Preservation –
    301-652-3377/www.parkwaydrycleaning.com

Vina Fabrics & Bridal – 301-439-0220

Virginia

Allegra's Bridal – 703-494-3293

Bobbie's Bridal Boutique – 703-273-2629/
    www.bobbiesbridal.com

Bridal Gown Restoration & Preservation Co. –
    703-573-8899, 800-wed-gown/www.gown.com

The Bridal Shoppe – 703-368-0694/
    www.thebridalshoppe.com

Bridal Visions – 703-237-0010/
    www.foreverybride.com

Bridals by Van Doren – 703-590-2628

Creative Headpieces – 703-360-7500

Elegance Inc. – 703-715-0738

Elegant Rochee's/Alterations – 703-751-7868/
    www.tailoredman.com

Ellie's Bridal Boutique – 703-683-8697

Formal Affair by Charlotte – 540-347-5126/
    www.charlottesformal.com

G Street Fabrics – Centerville – 703-818-8090 –
    Other VA locations/ www.gstreetfabrics.com

Gossypia – 703-836-6969/www.gossypia.com

GownPro-Preservation – 800-469-6776/
    www.ravefabricare.com

Hannelore's Bridal Boutique – 703-549-0387

Imperial Gown Restoration & Preservation Co. –
    703-573-4696, 800-WED-GOWN/
    www.gown.com

Jeanette's Bride N Tux Boutique – 703-369-1998/
    www.jeanettesbride.com

Jessica McClintock Bridal – 703-790-0016/
    www.jessicamcclintock.com

Lady Hamilton – 703-521-0990/
    www.ladyhamiltonbridal.com

Lamour Bridal – 703-751-5651

La Reve Bridal Inc. – 703-777-3757

Leesburg Tuxedo – 703-777-8822

Personally Yours – Discount Bridal
    Services/Preservation – 703-876-9784

Phillies Bridal Wearhouse – 703-912-7700

Philomen – 703-823-4022

Priscilla of Boston – 703-821-0167/
    www.priscillaofboston.com

Rosalin's Bridal Boutique – 703-532-0288

Skandia Formals & Bridals – 703-281-9196

White Swan Bridal Boutique – 703-255-9032/
    www.whiteswanbridal.com

District of Columbia

A Wedding Creation – 202-333-5762

Alex: Designer/Consignor (Alex Garcia) –
    202-296-2610/www.alexdesigns.com

Bené Millinery & Bridal Supplies – 202-722-0862

Champs Elysees – 202-333-2648

Diana's Couture & Bridal – 202-333-5689/
    www.dianascoutureandbridal.com

Haehie's Designing Salon – 202-965-5313

Lynelle Boutique – 202-223-4222/
    www.lynelleboutique.com

Rizik Bros., Inc. – 202-223-4050/www.riziks.com

Toast & Strawberries/Orig. Designs/Alterations –
    202-234-2424/www.toastandstrawberries.com

Vera Wang Bridal Boutique – 202-337-4201

Brooklyn: Kleinfeld – 718-765-8500/
    www.kleinfeldbridal.com

CAKES

Maryland

Cake of Cakes – 301-725-6129

Cakes Plus – 301-490-3600, 1-800-255-9122/ www.cakesplus.com

Clements Pastry Shop – 301-277-6300

Creative Cakes – 301-587-1599/ www.creativecakes.com

Custom Cake Design, LLC – 301-216-1100/ www.customcakedesign.com

Fancy Cakes by Leslie – 301-548-9390/ www.fancycakesbyleslie.com

Giant – 888-4MY-GIANT/www.giantfood.com

Occasional Cakes – 301-868-3640/ www.occasionalcakesinc.com

Rolling Pin Bakery – 301-699-9119

Smallwood Bakers – 301-932-7682

Something Extra Cakery – 301-921-9194/ www.somethingextracakery.com

Virginia

Alexandria Pastry Shop – 703-578-4144

Always the Best Baking Company – 703-802-4959

Cake Lore – 703-830-8163/www.cakelore.com

The Cakery – 703-590-2301

Cakes By Linda – 703-893-4782/ www.cakesbylinda.com

Cakes Unique – 703-553-0649/ www.cakes-unique.com

Celebration Flowers & Cakes – 540-636-4995, 888-311-9900/www.celebrationweddings.com

Creative Wedding Cakes – 703-281-1789

Fran's Cake & Candy Supplies – 703-352-1471

The Garden Kitchen – 703-494-2848/ www.gardenkitchen.com

Giant – 888-4MY-GIANT/www.giantfood.com

Heidelberg Pastry Shoppe – 703-527-8394/ www.heidelbergbakery.com

Once Upon a Cake – 703-641-0151/ www.onceuponacake.com

Pastryarts – Steve Klc/Colleen Apte – 703-312-0006/www.pastryarts.com

Patty Cakes – 703-354-0677

The Sweet Life – 703-750-3266/ www.thesweetlife.com

The Swiss Bakery and Pastry Shop – 703-569-3670

Terra Cocoa – 703-753-9563/www.terracocoa.com

Victorian Cakes – 703-249-0996/ www.victoriancakesonline.com

Wanda's Cake Decorating – 703-830-3866

The Wedding Loft (Holland Flowers) – 703-684-1865/www.weddingloft.com

Wegmans – www.wegmans.com

District of Columbia

Amernick-Palena's Bakery – 202-537-5855/ www.palenarestaurant.com

Fancy Cakes – 202-726-2163

Giant – 888-4MY-GIANT/www.giantfood.com

Heller's Bakery – 202-265-1190

New York: Sylvia Weinstock Cakes – 212-925-6698/www.sylviaweinstock.com

Alternative: Bundles of Cookies – 301-652-8840/ www.bundlesofcookies.com

CALLIGRAPHERS

Maryland

Calligraphy Graphic Design – 301-236-4973/ www.calligraphygraphicdesign.com

Calligraphy Services – 301-963-1431

Caren Milman Calligraphy – 301-871-6714

Creative Parties, Ltd. – 301-654-9292/ www.cparties.com

Folsom Calligraphy – 301-681-9688

McCann Calligraphy – 301-270-9001/ www.mcscribe.com

Sammy Little – 301-977-1554/
www.sammylittle.com

Virginia

Arts and Calligraphy – 703-941-2560

Jill Norvell Calligraphy – 703-264-0600

Personally Yours – 703-876-9784/
www.personallyyours.invitations.com

District of Columbia

Creative Script Inc. – 202-337-9377/
www.creativescript.invitations.com

David A. Hobbs, Inc. & Tolley Studios –
202-347-4411/www.wwco.com/hobbs

Inkwell Inc. – 202-234-8480/
www.inkwellcalligraphy.net

CATERERS

Maryland

C&E Catering – 301-590-6262/
www.cecatering.com

Catering by DoNia – 301-731-0639

Catering by Joyce – 301-670-2787/
www.cateringbyjoyce.com

Charles Levine Caterers – 410-363-0900/
www.gloriouskosher.com

Clements Pastry Shop – 301-277-6300

Corcoran Caterers Inc. – 301-588-9200/
www.corcorancaterers.com

Distinctive Catering – 866-802-1544/
www.distinctivecateringbyron.com

EatZi's Market & Bakery – 301-816-0330/
www.eatzis.com

Elegant Pantry – 301-770-5327/
www.epcaterers.com

Eric & Company – 301-460-6070

Federal City Caterers – 301-897-8181/
www.federalcitycaterers.com

Festive Foods Catering, Inc. – 301-230-2700/
www.festivefoods.com

Gail's Vegetarian Meals – 301-565-0674/
www.gailsvegetarian.com

Giant – 888-4MY-GIANT/www.giantfood.com

InStyle Caterers – 301-486-0300/
www.instylecaterers.com

J&L Caterers – 301-330-4735

Knife & Fork Caterers – 301-670-4744/
www.theknifeandfork.com

La Fontaine Bleu – 301-731-4333/
www.lafontainebleu.com

Luck's Catering – 301-468-3870

Mr. Omelette – 301-340-2800/
www.mromelettemd.com

Marco Polo Caterers – 301-299-2400/
www.marcopolocaterers.com

Martin's Crosswinds – 301-474-8500/
www.martinscaterers.com

Maryland Country Caterers – 800-362-1631/
www.marylandcountrycaterers.com

Med-Catering Corporation – 301-946-2230/
www.medcatering.com

The Pepperpot Cafe – 301-937-7676/
www.pepperpotcafe.com

The Perfect Grind – 301-762-7733

Pineapple Alley Catering – 301-856-1954/
www.pineapplealley.com

The Prime Choice Caterers – 301-948-7337/
www.theprimechoicecaterers.com

Provisions – 301-949-6100

Ridgewell's – 301-652-1515/www.ridgewells.com

Safeway – 1-877-SAFEWAY/www.safeway.com

Susan Gage – 301-839-6900

Sutton Place Gourmet – 301-564-3100/
www.suttongourmet.com

Whole Foods Market – www.wholefoods.com

Virginia

American Bar-B-Que & Catering – 703-550-7757/
www.americanbbq.com

Avalon Caterers, Intl. – 703-823-8829/
www.avaloncaterers.com

Better Events – 703-204-1800

Catering by Windows – 703-519-3500/
www.catering.com

Celebrations – 703-450-MMMM(6666)/
www.goldgrape.com

Design Cuisine – 703-979-9400/
www.designcuisine.com

Giant Gourmet Someplace Special –
703-448-0800/www.giantfood.com/catering

Heart in Hand Restaurant & Catering Company –
703-830-4111/www.heartinhandrestaurant.com

Helga's Caterers – 703-556-0780

J.R.'s Custom Catering – 703-821-0545/
www.jrsbeef.com

Marco Polo Caterers – 703-281-3922/
www.marcopolocaterers.com

Matters of Taste Caterers – 703-683-6555

Pampered Palate/Personal Chef & Catering
Service – 703-622-9269/
www.pamperedpalatepersonalchef.com

Panache Catering Company – 800-325-5586/
www.panachecatering.com

R&R Catering – 703-451-2798/
www.rrcatering.com

RSVP Catering – 703-573-8700/
www.rsvpcatering.com

Red Hot & Blue Catering – 1-888-509-7100/
www.redhotandblue.com

Safeway – 1-877-SAFEWAY/www.safeway.com

Sara McGregor's Capitol Catering –
703-739-1030/www.capitolcatering.com

Splendid Fare Catering – 703-519-1777

Sue Fischer Kosher Catering/Catering by
Windows – 703-519-8833/www.catering.com

Sutton Place Gourmet – 703-448-3828/
www.suttongourmet.com

Wegmans – www.wegmans.com

Whole Foods Market – www.wholefoods.com

District of Columbia

Avalon Caterers – 202-337-2000/
www.avaloncaterers.com

B&B Washington's Caterer – 202-829-8640/
www.washingtonscaterers.com

3 Citron Caterers – 202-342-3400/
www.3citron.com

Carole Ash's The Artful Party – 202-362-0268/
www.artfulparty.com

Catering by Uptown – 202-483-2058/
www.cateringbyuptown.com

Chateau Inc. – 202-399-0106

Classic Affairs – 202-543-4462/
www.classicaffairscatering.com

Cross Catering Service – 202-332-6599/
www.adelisdining.com

Dean & DeLuca – 1-202-342-2500

Federal City Caterers – 202-408-9700/
www.federalcitycaterers.com

fete accomplie catering inc. – 202-338-3383/
www.feteaccompliecatering.com

Fettoosh – 202-342-1199/www.fettoosh1.com

Foxhall Gourmet Deli (up to 75 persons) –
202-333-3444

Furin's of Georgetown – 202-965-1000/
www.furins.com

Giant – 888-4MY-GIANT/www.giantfood.com

Gist Family Catering Service – 202-722-5003/
www.gistfamilycatering.com

Gourmet To Go Catering – 202-361-6159/
www.thegourmettogo.com

Graceful Affairs Caterers – 202-667-6460/
www.gracefulaffairs.com

Grand Cuisine Caterers – 202-637-4926/
www.grandcuisinedc.com

The Grand Gourmet – 202-466-4665

Lawson's Gourmet Provisions – 202-789-1440

Lord's Caterers – 202-726-7134

Main Event Caterers – 202-463-7766/
www.maineventcaterers.com

Mindy's Catering Inc. – 202-342-6207

Napa Valley Caterers (George Velazquez) –
202-232-7816/www.napavalleycaterers.com

Occasions Caterers – 202-546-7400/
www.occasionscaterers.com

Paris Caterers – 202-635-3500/
www.pariscaterers.com

Quite A Stir Catering – 202-298-6818/
www.quiteastircatering.com

Rocklands Barbecue and Grilling Company –
202-333-2556/www.rocklands.com

Safeway – 1-877-SAFEWAY/www.safeway.com

Sans Rival Caterers – 202-462-4454

Sardis Catering Service – 202-293-5666

Sutton Place Gourmet – 202-363-5800/
www.suttongourmet.com

W. Millar & Co. – 202-387-2216/
www.wmillar.com

Well Dunn Catering Inc. – 202-543-7878/
www.welldunn.com

Whole Foods Market – www.wholefoods.com

Who's Cookin'? – 202-625-2671/
www.whoscookin.biz

Staff Only

The Daria Group – 301-315-8218

Food Temps – 301-230-9090/www.foodtemps.com

Kosher Catering Referral

The Rabbinical Council of Greater Washington –
202-291-6052/
www.capitolk.org/supervised/caterers.html

Personal Chefs

Eat-In-Chef/Chef Tom DeBlois – 703-585-2893
(up to 25 persons/buffet)

The Pampered Palate/Chef Tony DeWalt –
703-622-9269/
www.pamperedpalatepersonalchef.com

ENTERTAINMENT

Maryland

About Faces Entertainment – 1-800-92-FUNNY

Absolute Entertainment/DJ – 1-800-252-5274/
www.absoluteentertainment.com

Bialek's Music – 301-340-6206/
www.bialeksmusic.com

Black Tie Arts Management – 301-532-7200

Bruce Ewan and the Solid Senders – 301-593-1348

Chamber Music Unlimited – 301-846-0855

Crystal Strings – 301–464-2828

Davis Deejays – 1-888-DAVIS-DJ

Doc Scantlin – 301-855-9102/
www.docscantlin.com

Entertainment Exchange – 888-238-2343,
410-828-0305/www.entertainmentexchange.com

Fantasy World Entertainment – 800-757-6332/
www.fwworld.com

Glen Pearson Productions & Floating Opera –
301-585-8579/www.pearsonproductions.com

Good Vibrations – 1-800-823-4656/
www.goodvibrations.org

Steve Hoffman/DJ – 301-270-8520

Bob Israel Entertainment Services – 301-704-4314

The Jim Bowie Band – 301-972-8365/
www.jimbowieband.com

Latin American Music Company – 410-685-4198

Mr. B/DJ – 301-372-8604

Mid-Atlantic Professional DJ Association –
1-800-795-1808/www.mapdja.com

Mixmaster Entertainment/DJ-Brian Glaser –
301-567-2738

Music Unlimited – 301-948-5419/
www.musicunlimited.com

NYX Entertainment – 301-984-0500/
www.nyxentertainment.com

Night & Day – 301-593-4209/
www.nightanddaymusic.com

Peaches O'Dell and her Orchestra – 301-897-8000

Potomac Talent, LLC – 301-587-6767

Retrospect – 301-831-5700/
www.retrospectband.com

Richard Bray Orchestras – 301-946-2729

Starlite Strings – 301-983-1257

Dick Steiner Magical Entertainer – 410-987-7801

Strolling Singer - Merv Conn – 301-565-2054

The Strolling Strings – 301-292-2929/
www.thestrollingstrings.com

Talk of the Town Entertainment – 301-738-9500

THEPROS (DJ) – 1-800-843-7767/
www.thepros.biz

Ultimate Entertainment, Inc. – 301-840-9021,
1-800-PARTY61/
www.ultimate-entertainment.com

Washington Talent Agency – 301-762-1800/
www.washingtontalent.com

Wright Music and Productions – 301-292-0584

Virginia

BB&C Productions – 703-522-4277

Black Tie Arts Management – 703-532-7200

Black Tie DJ's – 703-803-7722/www.musicdj.com

Joe Blumka-Accordian – 703-931-9335

Capital Entertainment & Music–- 703-836-9390/
www.capitalentertainment.biz

Carousel Puppets – 703-444-9426/
www.carouselpuppets.com

Cast of Thousands – 703-442-8400/
www.castof1000s.com

Christian & Company Entertainment –
703-425-6663/www.gr8shows.com

Con Brio Chamber Music – 703-938-5086

Elan Artists – 1-800-933-7917/
www.elanartists.com

The Gypsy Strings – 703-273-0544

Harp Music by Lucinda Caldwell – 703-768-1531

MSE Productions – 703-620-5554/
www.mseproductions.com

Mariachi Los Amigos – 703-671-5463

Meray Entertainment – 703-360-5240

Olivera Music & Entertainment – 703-724-0505

Riverside Brass – 703-575-9480/
www.welgoss.com/riverside

Mark Sonder Productions – 703-968-8670/
www.marksonderproductions.com

Stereo Strings – Lou Coppola – 703-379-7400/
www.stereostrings.com

Strolling Singer/Accordianist/Gretchen –
703-847-9400

Soundwave Entertainment/DJ – 703-233-2599/
www.soundwavedj.com

Rod Tompkins Music – 703-768-6448/
www.rodmusic.com

District of Columbia

Joe Burden – 202-726-6433, 800-246-6986

Dave Burns Music – 202-462-2129

Eric Felton Jazz Orchestra – 202-338-1999

Bill Harris/Pianist – 202-296-8102

New Legacy Jazz Band – 1-800-807-9464

Now This – 202-364-8292

Sidney's Music & Entertainment – 202-223-3007

Trinidad & Tobago Steel Band Organization of
Washington – 202-745-9150

Washington's Best Musicians – 202-232-4942

Benjamin Waters Music – 1-800-793-6722

EQUIPMENT RENTAL

Maryland

Allied Rentals – 301-986-0067

Capital Party Rentals – 301-231-9600,
800-736-8253/www.capitalrentals.com

Classic Tents – 301-588-3181

Fandango – 410-539-7236/
www.fandangoevents.com

Gaithersburg Party Rental Center – 301-963-9011/
www.gaithersburg-rentals.com

Gala Cloths by Dulany – 1-888-747-1144

Gala Events, Inc. – 301-718-2900/
www.galaevents.com

Grand Rental Station – 410-674-7500/
www.partyandtentrentals.com

Hargrove, Inc. – 301-306-9000, 888-790-9792/
www.hargroveinc.com

HDO Productions (Tents) – 301-881-8700/
www.hdotents.com

Loane Bros (Tents) – 410-686-9200

Magic Rainbow Rentals – 301-408-3096

Party Cloths, Etc. – 301-608-3600/
www.partycloths.com

Party Perfect (Tents, tables & chairs) –
800-400-7610/www.perfectparties.com

Party Rental Ltd. – 301-931-4580/
www.partyrentalltd.com

Ridgewell's Caterer Rental Division –
301-652-1515/www.ridgewells.com

Sugarplum Tent Company – 301-869-2054/
www.sugarplumtents.com

Select Event Rentals – 301-937-7600,
410-653-6851/www.weparty.com

Virginia

A Plus Rental Center – 703-451-6060/
www.aplusrental.com

Alexandria Rent-All Center – 703-780-8374/
www.rentallcenter.com

Brooke Rental Center, Inc. – 703-938-4807/
www.brookerental.com

Capital Party Rentals – 703-278-8300,
800-736-8253/www.capitalrentals.com

Chantilly Event Rentals – 703-378-2255/
www.eventrentals.com

DC Rental – 1-800-778-7368/www.dcrental.com

District of Columbia

FanFair (Patio/Deck Fans) – 202-342-6290

Perfect Settings – 202-722-2900, 888-569-2900/
www.perfectsettings.com

EVENT PLANNERS

Maryland

Bonnie Schwartz & Company – 301-229-9473/
www.bonnieschwartz.com

Creative Parties – 301-654-9292/www.cparties.com

Distinctive Events by Susan B. Katz, Inc. –
301-933-7700/www.susanbkatz.com

Ellen Dubin – 301-983-3414

Extraordinary Events – 301-631-2425

Finishing Touches Events – 301-718-6465/
www.finishingtouchesevents.com

For Your Special Day – 301-589-8650/
www.foryourspecialday.com

Gala Events, Inc. – 301-718-2900/
www.galaevents.com

Hargrove Inc. – 301-306-9000, 888-790-9792/
www.hargroveinc.com

Occasions, Etc. – 301-520-0341/
www.occasionsetc.com

P.W. Feats, Inc. – 410-727-5575

Wendy Katzen "Party Perfect" – 301-299-9334/
www.wendykatzen.com

Arlene Perkins – 301-670-0544

Rave Reviews – 301-933-7989/
www.4ravereviews.com

Ray-Al Wedding Consulting – 301-604-1308

Save The Date Inc. – 301-983-6222

Signature Events – 301-320-5433

Simax Event Production – 301-601-8006

Singer Associates Event Management –
301-365-2636

Smooth Weddings – 301-972-5233/
www.smoothweddings.com

Super Soirees, Ltd. – 301-983-1910/
www.joannew.net

Tying The Knot – 301-384-7015

Virginia

A Perfect Wedding – 703-691-0133/
www.aperfectwed.com

Albright Events.Inc. – 703-879-6931/
www.albrightevents.com

Allure Events, Inc. – 703-550-1310/
www.anallureevent.com

BB&C Productions – 703-522-4277

Capitol Events – 703-575-3430/
www.capitolevents.com

Capitol Services, Inc. – 703-584-2460/
www.csi-dc.com

Classic Celebrations – 703-368-0496

Dave Edwards Eventz! – 703-812-0525

Elegant Engagements – 703-819-5808/
www.elegantengagements.com

Engaging Affairs – 1-888-481-5156

Event Consultants, Inc. – 703-941-7549

Hunt Country Celebrations – 540-347-4414,
800-820-1021/
www.huntcountrycelebrations.com

Northern Virginia Bridal Services – 703-516-4732/
www.novabridal.com

On-Site Productions,Inc. – 703-299-500l/
www.on-siteproductions.com

PGI Washington – 703-528-8484/www.PGI.com

The Party Portfolio – 703-356-3050/
www.partyportfolio.com

Precision Meetings & Events – 703-739-4480/
www.teamprecision.com

Romantic Betrothal (Sara Franco) – 703-644-8462

Washington, Inc/PGI – 703-528-8484/
www.PGI.com

The Wedding Loft (Holland Flowers) –
703-684-1865/www.weddingloft.com

District of Columbia

Bralove/Hollman Special Events – 202-363-9833/
www.bhevents.com

Eventions By Rhonda – 202-479-0855

Jodi Moraru & Associates – 202-237-8244/
www.jodimoraru.com

Susan Davis International – 202-408-0808/
www.susandavis.com

USA Hosts – 202-857-4111/www.usahosts.com

San Francisco: Stanlee Gatti Designs –
415-558-8884/www.stanleegatti.com

FLOWERS

Maryland

AJ Designs – 301-984-0588

Behnke Nursery – 301-983-4400/
www.behnkes.com

Bethesda Florist, Inc. – 301-656-8200/
www.bethesdaflorist.com

Encore Décor – 301-565-0020

Exquisite Design Studio – 301-951-8109/
www.exquisitefloral.com

Floral Affairs – 301-565-0020

Floral Events Unlimited – 301-585-2772

Flowers by Angels – 301-528-5114

Flowers World Wide – 301-948-6667/
www.areaflorist.com

Foxglove Design – 410-244-1369/
www.foxglovedesign.com

Giant – 1-888-4MY-GIANT/www.giantfood.com

Nelsons Flower Shoppe – 301-869-2400/
www.nelsonsflowershoppe.com

Rockville Floral & Garden Spot – 301-984-3563/
www.rockvilleflowergarden.com

Safeway – 1-877-SAFEWAY/www.safeway.com

John Sharper, Inc. Florist – 301-567-4600/
www.sharperflorist.com

Sutton Place Gourmet/www.suttongourmet.com

Vince's Agnes Flower Shop, Inc. – 301-588-8484/
www.vinceagnesflowershop.com

Virginia

Accolades Florist – 703-492-9732

Alexandria Floral Company – 703-549-0400/
www.alexandriafloral.com

Art With Flowers – 703-903-6837

Blooming Spaces – 703-435-1882/
www.bloomingspaces.com

Blooms – 703-620-5557, 1-800-441-2566,
www.blooms.com

Buckingham Florists – 703-525-6222/
www.buckinghamfloristofarlington.com

Classic Flowers & Gifts – 703-451-1515/
www.classicflowersandgifts.com

Company Flowers & Gifts – 703-525-3062/
www.companyflowers.com

Conklyn's Florist – 703-299-9000/
www.conklyns.com

Distinctive Floral Designs – 703-430-0312/
www.distinctivefloral.com

Enchanted Florist – 703-549-0012

Flowers Unique by Marchand – 703-548-4638

Giant – 1-888-4MY-GIANT/www.giantfood.com

Green Mansions Florist – 1-800-278-2642

The Growing Wild Floral Company –
540-364-6246

Holland Flowers – 703-684-1865/
www.weddingloft.com

JLB Floral – 703-751-4031

Jack Lucky Floral Design. Inc. – 703-533-1515/
www.jackluckyfloraldesign.com

McLean Gray Matter Florist, Ltd. – 703-356-5100/
www.graymatterflorist.com

Michael's Flowers & Gifts – 703-451-3021/
www.michaelsflowers.net

Multiflor – 703-734-6720/www.nicksflowers.com

Ritz Carlton Floral Department – 703-412-3794

Safeway – 1-877-SAFEWAY/www.safeway.com

Sutton Place Gourmet – www.suttongourmet.com

Wegmans – www.wegmans.com

Wilson Florist of Rosslyn – 703-525-7792/
www.wilsonfloristofrosslyn.com

Wisteria – 703-548-3111

Yellow Door Floral Design – 703-237-5350

District of Columbia

Allan Woods, Florist – 202-332-3334/
www.allanwoods.com

Amaryllis, Inc. – 202-289-8535/
www.amaryllisflowers.com

Aster Florist – 202-387-0092/
www.asterflowers.com

Sue Bluford Floral Designs – 202-723-9172

Capitol Hill Flowers and Fruit – 202-547-7355/
www.capitolhills.com

Caruso's Florist – 202-223-3816/
www.carusoflorist.net

Flowers by Sandra – 202-223-2920

Friendship Flower Shop – 202-966-4405/
www.friendshipflowers.com

Giant – 1-888-4MY-GIANT/www.giantfood.com

Greenworks – 202-265-3335/
www.greenworksflorist.com

Johnson's Flower & Garden Center –
202-244-6100/www.johnsonsflowers.com

Lee's Flower & Card Shop – 202-265-4965/
www.leesflowerandcard.com

Lola's Flower Garden – 202-483-2052

Mayflower Floral Decorators – 202-776-9113/
www.mayflowerfloraldecorators.com

The Ociana Group – 202-269-0044

Palace Florists, Inc. – 202-833-1095/
www.palaceflorists.com

Renae's Flowers & Gifts, Inc. – 202-678-1785/
www.renaesflowers.com

Safeway – 1-877-SAFEWAY/www.safeway.com

Sutton Place Gourmet/www.suttongourmet.com

ULTRA Violet Flowers – 202-333-3002/
www.ultravioletflowersdc.com

Washington Floral Design Group – 202-269-5701

San Francisco: Stanlee Gatti Designs –
415-558-8884/www.stanleegatti.com

Pick Your Own Flowers
Maryland

Butler's Orchard – 301-972-3299/
www.butlersorchard.com

Frank's Produce – 410-799-4566

Farmhouse Flowers & Plants – 301-963-5044/
www.farmhouseflowers.com

Virginia

Fields of Flowers – 540-338-7231

Silk Flowers

J. Brown & Company – 703-548-9010

Balloons

Balloons 'n More – 301-589-8144

Beautiful Balloons – 301-468-5533

Exquisite Balloons – 301-924-4516/
www.exquisiteballoons.com

Fantastic Inflations – 703-690-9575

Magical & Memorable Balloons – 301-490-8935/
www.magicalmemorableballoons.com

Alternatives & Additions

Ice Kristals – 703-369-7374/www.icekristals.com

Plants Alive (Large Plants & Trees Rentals) –
301-598-3843

Preservation

Forever Yours – 410-768-9565/
www.foreveryoursmd.com

GIFTS, FAVORS AND NOVELTIES

Maryland

A Glorious Occasion – 301-929-1834

Balloons 'n More – 301-589-8144

Beautiful Balloons – 301-468-5533

Bundles of Cookies – 301-652-8840/
www.bundlesofcookies.com

Capital Gifts & Awards – 301-970-1989/
www.capitalgifts.com

Exquisite Balloons – 301-924-4516

Linganore Winecellars – 301-831-5889/
www.linganore-wine.com

Magical & Memorable Balloons, Inc. –
301-490-8935/
www.magicalmemorableballoons.com

The Ad Solution – 301-231-8600, ext.109/
www.adsolution.com

Virginia

Arts Afire – 703-838-9785/www.artsafire.com

J. Brown & Company – 703-548-9010

Egerton Gardens – 703-548-1197/
www.egerton-gardens.com

Elements – 703-490-8697

My Place in Tuscany – 800-261-5407/
www.myplaceintuscany.com

The Occoquan Basket Co. – 877-266-1806/
www.occoquanbasketco.com

Prezzies – 703-442-4575

Quinn's Goldsmith – 703-494-1662/
www.quinnsgold.com

Shirley's Gift Baskets – 703-802-2834

Wilfred-Rodgers – 703-548-4543

District of Columbia

Dolly Kay at The Tiny Jewel Box – 202-393-2747/
www.tinyjewelbox.com

Elite Occasions/Gift Baskets – 202-342-2111

ID Partners/Mark Solomon –
866-255-2220, ext. 12/
www.idpartnersonline.com

Martin's of Georgetown – 202-338-6144

Region-Wide

www.bloomingdales.com

www.brookstone.com

www.crateandbarrel.com

www.hechts.com

www.homedepot.com

www.jcpenney.com

www.kmart.com

www.kohls.com

www.lordandtaylor.com – 800-223-7440 (for Store Locations)

www.macys.com

www.neimanmarcus.com

www.potterybarn.com

www.replacements.com/info/bridal.html – REPLACEMENTS, (China,Silver) – 1-800-REPLACE

www.restorationhardware.com

www.saks.com – Saks Fifth Avenue – 1-800-331-6552

www.sears.com

www.sharperimage.com

www.target.com

www.williamssonoma.com

GROOM'S ATTIRE/FORMAL WEAR

Maryland

After Hours Formal Wear – 1-800-616-8897/ www.afterhours.com

Allurs Formal Wear – 301-702-8717

Annapolis Formal – 410-266-6262

Athens Men's Formal Wear Rental – 410-719-8819

Bethesda Custom Tailors & Formal Wear – 301-656-2077/www.bethesdatailors.com

Catonsville Tuxedo Company – 410-747-2255

Charelle's Costume & Tuxedo Shoppe – 301-695-6543

Cy's of Catonsville – 410-747-8760

Jim Dandy Tuxedo Rentals – 301-585-6810

Gage World Class Men's Store – 410-727-0763

Gamberdella Formal Wear – 410-828-0707

Gingiss formalwear – 1-877-816-6060/ www.gingiss.com

J's Custom Tailoring & Formal Wear – 301-652-8852

K & G Super Store – 410-594-9700/ www.kgstore.com

King's Contrivance Formal Wear & Custom Tailoring Inc. – 410-381-0619

Masters Tuxedo – 1-800-572-3353/ www.masterstuxedo.com

Menswarehouse – 1-800-851-6744/ www.menswarehouse.com

Mode Custom Tailor Shop – 301-474-2004

Royal Formal Wear ("We Come To You") – 1-800-433-3383

Snyder's Tuxedos, Inc. – 410-655-6611

Tuxedo Junction – 301- 449-4465

Your Custom Tailor – 301-694-0130

Virginia

After Hours Formal Wear – 1-800-616-8897/ www.afterhours.com

Allegra's Bridal – 703-494-3293

Carlton for Men – 540-373-0023

Elegant Rochees/Hong Kong Tailors – 703-751-7868

Formal Affair – 540-347-5126

Gingiss Formalwear – 1-877-816-6060/ www.gingiss.com

Hannelore's Bridal Boutique – 703-549-0387

Harvard Men's Wear, Inc. – 703-671-9255

Hodas Formal Wear – 540-898-5039

Jeannette's Bride N Tux Boutique – 703-369-1998/ www.jeanettesbride.com

Kapfer Tailoring Ltd. – 703-352-5202

King's Park Tailoring – 703-425-2064

Le Reve Bridal & Tuxedo – 703-777-3757

Leesburg Bridal & Tuxedo – 703-777-8822

Masters Tuxedo – 1-800-572-3353/
www.masterstuxedo.com

Pervins Custom Tailor & Formal Wear –
703-404-9051

Royal Formal Wear ("We Come To You") –
1-800-433-3383

Suh's Custom Tailors & Tuxedo – 703-802-9636,
Alex. 703-836-2130

District of Columbia

After Hours Formal Wear – 1-800-616-8897/
www.afterhours.com

Anthony's Tuxedo – 202-333-5762

Baytok's Custom Tailor – 202-337-4800

Capitol Hill Tailor Shop – 202-543-9292

Christopher Kim's Men's Wear & Tailoring –
202-955-5467

Gingiss formalwear – 877-816-6060/
www.gingiss.com

Highcliffe Clothiers Ltd. – 202-872-8640

Lucas Tuxedo – 202-625-7108

Lustre Formal Wear of Capitol Hill –
202-544-0002

Masters Tuxedo – 1-800-572-3353/
www.masterstuxedo.com

Menswarehouse – 1-800-851-6744/
www.menswarehouse.com

Professional Man– 202-466-6255

Royal Formal Wear ("We Come To You") –
1-800-433-3383

Sauro Custom Tailoring – 202-296-0748

Scogna Formal Wear – 202-296-4555

M. Stein & Company – 202-659-1434

INVITATIONS/ANNOUNCEMENTS

Maryland

American Printing – 301-322-3500

Baumgarten Company of Washington –
301-317-3933

Creative Parties Ltd. – 301-654-9292/
www.cparties.com

Discount Invitations by Estelle – 301-460-1981

Fine Point Press – 410-266-8424/
www.finepointpress.com

The Perfect Note – 301-257-4577

The PROS – 1-800-843-7767/www.thepros.biz

Quick Printing – 301-949-3090

Rose Leaves – 301-493-5554

Sincerely Yours – 301-340-1989

Waldorf Engraving & Printing Co. –
301-843-7165, 301-645-0320

The Write Image – 301-896-0975/
www.thewriteimage.com

Virginia

A-3 Vision Production – 703-440-4000/
www.trivision.TV

Greetings & Salutations – 703-548-6690/
www.greetingssalutations.invitations.com

Hawthorne House – 703-491-5775/
www.hawthornehouse.cceasy.com

Invitation Connection – 703-998-3350,
888-988-5055/www.invitationconnection.com

Noteworthy Papers – 703-670-0030

Personally Yours – 703-876-9784/
www.personallyyours.invitations.com

The Wedding Loft (Holland Flowers) –
703-684-1865/www.weddingloft.com

Wrap It Up – 703-281-4329/
www.wrapitup.invitations.com

District of Columbia

A Wedding Creation – 202-333-5762

Advanced Printing – 202-898-1844

Baumgarten Company of Washington –
202-347-3933

Bethesda Engravers Limited – 202-331-0550

Brewood Engravers – 202-223-2300

Copenhaver – 202-232-1200

Creative Script – 202-337-9377/
www.creativescript.invitations.com

Distinctive Bookbinding – 202-466-4866

Downs Engravers & Stationers – 202-223-7776

Premier Printing & (In Home) Services –
202-635-2121, 800-282-2076

Washington Engraving Company – 202-638-3100/
www.washingtonengraving.com

Write For You – 202-686-7060

The Written Word – 202-223-1400/
www.writtenword.invitations.com

LIGHTING AND SOUND

Atmosphere, Inc. – 301-585-2100

Digital Lighting – 301-468-6440/
www.digitallighting.org

Frost Lighting – 703-866-5153/
www.frostlighting.com

Kinetic Artistry, Inc. – 301-270-6666

Permere Presentation (sound) – 703-204-1258

PHOTOGRAPHERS/VIDEOGRAPHERS

Maryland

Alan Photography – 301-977-2651

Clay Blackmore Photography – 301-670-3232/
www.clayblackmore.com

Blanken Photography Studios – 301-320-8714

Thomas Bowen Video – 301-294-5300/
www.bowenvideo.com

Brooks Glogau Studio – 301-654-1078/
www.glogau.com

Chase Photography – 301-986-1050

Vince Cowan Photographers – 301-585-1930/
www.vincecowan.com

Carl Cox Photography – 301-670-0086/
www.carlcoxphoto.com

Event Digital Photography – 301-229-3305/
www.eventdigital.com

Paul B. Fleming Photography – 301-990-9294/
www.pfleming.net

Freed Photography – 301-652-5452/
www.freedphoto.com

Larry Glatt – 301-929-0309

J. Stewart Harris Photography – 301-593-0627

Les Henig Photography – 301-933-5762/
www.leshenig.com

Susan Hornyuk – 301-263-0349

Image Perfect – 301-571-5240/
wwww.image-perfect.com

Robert Isacson – 301-299-0800/
www.isacsonstudios.com

Greg Kelly, Photographer – 301-977-8922/
www.gregkellyart.com

Michael B. Kress Photography – 301-654-0909/
www.michaelkressphotography.com

Howard Lansat – 301-838-9560/
www.lansatphoto.com

Jenny Lehman Videographer – 301-567-9622/
www.videojournalist.com

MH Concepts – 301-947-3430/
www.mhconcepts.com

On Line Suburban Video, Inc. – 301-315-6300/
www.suburbanvideo.com

On Q'ue Photography – 301-699-8677/
www.onqphoto.com

THE PROS – 1-800-843-7767/www.thepros.biz

Rez Video Art – 301-371-8927

Don Roberts, Videographer – 301-948-8860/
www. acevid.com

Barbara Saks-Kanegis – 301-625-0300

Spero's Video – 301-277-3357/
www.sperosvideo.com

Stone Photography – 301-654-3185/
www.stonephotography.com

Studio One – 301-652-1345/
www.photographycenter.com

Taylor-Made Video Production – 301-445-2171

Video Express Productions – 301-598-6096/
www.videoexpresspro.com

Visions In Photography, Inc. – 301-279-2451/
www.visionsinphotography.com

George Weller Photographer/Videographer –
301-977-7471

Robert T. Williams/Photojournalist –
301-429-0692/www.robertwilliams.com

Virginia

Bachrach Photographers – 703-548-2111/
www.bachrachinc.com

Matt Barrett – 703-644-7104/
www.erols.com/mbphoto

Philip Bermingham Portrait Photography –
703-827-5957/www.philipbermingham.com

Bright Star Productions (Video) – 703-818-0056/
www.brightstarvideo.com

Celebration Photography – 703-869-7869/
www.hutzell.com

Creation Waits – 703-243-0536/
www.creationwaits.com

Creative Arts Photography – l-800-722-1399/
www.creativefoto.com

Focused Images Photography, Inc. – 703-435-3456/
www.focusedimages.com

Hill Signature Portraits – 703-759-9550/
www.hillsignature.com

Marty LaVor – 703-765-7187/www.martylavor.com

Ernesto Maldonado – 888-621-3609/
www.emphotography.com

Naltchayan Photography – 703-533-2424

Photographic Services of Alexandria, Inc. –
703-548-0505

Photovision – 703-437-8366/www.photovis.com

Picture Perfect Weddings – 703-440-4086/
www.pictureperfectweddings.com

PictureProse – 703-658-7132

Studio M, Inc. (Video) – 703-471-4666

Sonshine Pictures – 540-349-8099/
www.sonshinepictures.com

Jenny Talati Tinius – 703-941-4028

Tessmer of Fairfax – 703-941-8270

Photography by Tisara Inc. – 703-838-8098/
www.tisaraphoto.com

Steve Tuttle Photography – 703-751-3452

Mark Vyrros – 703-715-0276

District of Columbia

Ashley Photographic Studios – 202-234-7879

Richard Basch Studio – 202-232-3100/
www.richardbasch.com

Jim Bradshaw Photographs – 202-575-2223

Leslie Cashan Photography – 202-363-5682

De Kun Photo – 202-337-3220

Earl Howard Studios – 202-582-1100/
www.earlhowardstudios.com

Jason Miccolo Johnson Photography –
202-387-6525/www.miccolo.com

Professional Image Photography/John Drew –
202-635-8801/www.professionalimage.com

Quality Photography – 202-543-5582

Robinson Photography – 202-832-5984

The Photographers Gallery – 202-362-8111/
www.thephotographersgallery.net

W.E. - VDO (Video) – 202-332-6804

Wedding Photography by Federico –
202-363-4528

TRANSPORTATION

Maryland

Imperial Limousines Inc. – 410-269-0000/
www.imperiallimos.com

Limousine's Inc. – 301-249-9466, 800-652-8224/
www.limos-inc.com

RMA Chauffeured Transportation –
301-231-6555/www.rmalimo.com

Virginia

A Limo Service, Inc. – 703-266-8709/
www.limousineservicecenter.com

Alabaster's Rolls Royce Weddings – 703-643-2678/
www.rollsweddings.com

Always A Pleasure Limousine, Inc. – 703-406-9697

Carey Worldwide Chauffeured Services –
703-892-2000, 800-622-5466

E Street Limousine – 703-938-5900/
www.estreetlimo.com

Harmon's Carriages/Meadow Acres Farm –
540-825-4688/www.cadcol.com/harmons

Regal Limousine Service – 703-440-3651

SI Services International Limousine & Travel –
703-506-9495/www.silimo.com

District of Columbia

Atlantic Services Group – 202-466-5050/
www.atlanticservicesgroup.com

Charley Horse Carriage Company – 202-488-1155

Limousines For You – 202-460-2595

Reston Limousine Service – 202-797-0500/
www.restonlimousine.com

VENUES

BOXED KEYS

C: - **Capacity:** Figures shown indicate maximum guests, usually combining indoor/outdoor space and for a reception/buffet. Seated capacity is generally less. Always check directly with the venue. Many configuration options are available, depending on the event.

Call - Contact vendor directly for capacity

cws - Call or check web site for capacity

ID - Indoors

OD - Outdoors

+ - Additional space/depends on circumstances, generally combination of ID/OD space

Maryland

Argyle Country Club – Silver Spring –
301-598-5500/www.argylecc.net/C: 250

The Ballroom – Bethesda – 301-913-9810/
www.theballroom.org/C: **cws**

Belair Mansion-Bowie – 301-809-3089/C: 75

Belmont Conference Center – Elkridge –
410-796-4300/www.acs.org/belmont/C: 80 **ID**/
1500 **OD**

Bethesda Marriott Hotel – 301-897-9400/
www.marriotthotels.com/C: **cws**

Blair Mansion Inn – Silver Spring – 301-588-1688/
C: **Call**

The Brome-Howard Inn – St. Mary's City –
301-866-0656/ www.bromehowardinn.com/
C: 120 **ID**/500 **OD**

Brookside Gardens – Wheaton – 301-962-1404/
www.brooksidegardens.org/C: **cws**

Build-A-Bear Workshop at Westfield
Shoppingtown – 301-365-8388/
www.buildabear.com/C: **Call**

Ceresville Mansion – Frederick – 301-694-5111/
www.ceresville.com/C: 200 **+**

The Claridge Room (Kensington/Wheaton) –
301-946-2517/C: 325

Clyde's Chevy Chase Race Bar – 301-951-9600/
www.clydes.com/C: **Call**

Clyde's – Columbia – 410-730-2829/
www.clydes.com/C: **Call**

Darnall's Chance – Upper Marlboro –
301-952-8010/C: **Call**

Dave & Buster's – White Flint – 301-230-5151/
www.daveandbusters.com/C: **cws**

DoubleTree Hotel Rockville – 301-468-1100/
www.doubletreehotels.com/C: **cws**

The Elkridge Furnace Inn – 410-379-9336/
www.elkridgefurnaceinn.com/C: 200

Forest Oak Lodge #123 Knights of Pythias –
Gaithersburg – 301-926-9263/C: 299

Four Points by Sheraton – 301-654-1000/
www.fourpoints.com/bethesda/C: 200

The Fraternal Order of Eagles Banquet Room –
Gaithersburg – 301-258-9344 /www.foe.com/
C: 175

Gaithersburg Hilton – 301-977-8900/
www.hiltons.com/C: **cws**

Glenview Mansion at Rockville Civic Center Park
– 240-314-8660/C: 225

Golden Bull Grand Café – Gaithersburg –
301-948-3666/C: 300

Governor Calvert House – Annapolis –
410-263-2641/C: **Call**

Holiday Inn – Bethesda – 301-652-2000/
www.holiday-inn.com/C: **cws**

Holiday Inn – Chevy Chase – 301-656-1500
/www.holiday-inn.com/C: 250

Holiday Inn – Gaithersburg – 301-948-8900/
www.holiday-inn.com/C: 300

Holiday Inn – Silver Spring – 301-589-0800/
www/holiday-inn.com/C: 300

The Inn at Buckeystown – 301-874-5755,
1-800-272-1190/
www.innatbuckeystown.com/C:175

Izora Restaurant & Night Club – Silver Spring –
301-495-2960/ www.izora.net/C: 300

Kentlands Mansion – Gaithersburg –
301-258-6425/C: 120

LaFerme – Chevy Chase – 301-986-5255/C: 200

Mrs. K's Toll House Restaurant – Silver Spring –
301- 589-3500/www.mrs-ks.com/C: 60

Made By You, Bethesda – 301-654-3206/C: **Call**

Made By You, Rockville – 301-610-5496/C: **Call**

Martins Crosswinds – Greenbelt –
301-474-8500/C: **Call**

McCrillis Gardens – Bethesda – 301-962-1400/
www.brooksidegardens.org/C: **cws OD**

Newton White Mansion – Mitchellville –
301-249-2004/www.pgparks.com/C: 250

Nixon's Farm – West Friendship –
1-800-942-4509/C: 2500 **OD**

Norbeck Country Club – Rockville –
301-774-7700/www.norbeckcc.com/C: 200

Normandie Farm – Potomac – 301-983-8838/
www.normandiefarm.com /C: **cws**

Oakland Historic Mansion – Columbia –
410-730-4801/C: 150 **ID**/200 **OD**

Oxon Hill Manor – 301-839-7782/
www.oxonhillmanor.org/C: 300

Party Places.Maryland – www.childrenparty.com/
partyplaces/marylandlist.html/C: **Call**

Positano Ristorante – Bethesda – 301-654-1717/
C: 150

Potomac Valley Lodge – Poolesville –
301-428-8283/C: 200 **ID**/4000 **OD**

Prince George's Ballroom – Landover –
301-341-7439/C: 250

Prince George's Sports & Learning Complex –
Landover – 301-583-2400/
www.pgsportsandlearn.com/C: **Call**

Quality Suites Shady Grove – Rockville –
301-840-0200/C: 350

Rockwood Manor Park – Potomac –
301-299-5026/ www.rockwoodmanor.com/C:175

The Rose Room – Bethesda – 301-652-2278/
www.bccrs.org/C: 600

Rossborough Inn– College Park – 301-314-8013/
C: 150 **ID**/200 **OD**

Savage Mill/Great Room – Savage –
1-800-213-7427/C: Mill 110/Great Room 275

Silver Diner – Several Locations –
www.silverdiner.com

Smokey Glen Farm – Gaithersburg –
301-948-9170/C: **Call OD**

Stone Manor – Middletown – 301-473-5454/
www.stonemanor.com/C: **cws**

Strathmore Hall Arts Center – North Bethesda –
301-530-5889/ www.strathmore.org/C: 225

Timpano – Rockville – 301-881-7058/C: 100

Treetops Atrium – Landover – 301-918-4000, 301-
577-3300/ www.treetopsatrium.com/C: **cws**

Watermark Cruises – Annapolis – 301-261-2719/ www.watermarkcruises.com/C: **Call**

Waverly Mansion – Marriottsville – 410-313-5400/ C: **Call**

Weddings on the Water – Annapolis/Baltimore – 301-261-2719/ www.annapoliscruises.com/C: **Call**

William Paca House – Annapolis – 410-263-5553/ C: **Call**

The Willow Tree Inn – Gaithersburg – 301-948-8832/C: **Call**

Woodend – Chevy Chase – 301-652-9188/C: 150

Woodlawn Manor – Sandy Spring – 301-299-5026/ C: 125 **ID**/250 **OD**

Virginia

2941 Restaurant – Falls Church – 703-270-1511/ www.2941restaurant.com/C: 80 **ID**/100**+ OD**

Airlie Center – Warrenton – 540-347-1300, 1-800-288-9573/www.airlie.com/C:50 **ID**/225 **OD**

Ashburn Ice House – 703-858-0300/ www.ashburnice.com/C: 400

The Atrium at Meadowlark Gardens – Vienna – 703-255-3631, ext. 104/C: 300

The Bailiwick Inn – Fairfax City – 703-691-2266, 1-800-366-7666/www.bailiwickinn.com/ C: 85

The Barns at Wolf Trap (Limited availability/ space) – Vienna – 703-938-8463/Call for specific information

Bristow Manor – 703-368-3558, ext. 28/C: 250

Build-A-Bear Workshop at Fair Oaks – 703-383-3140/www.buildabear.com/C: **Call**

Build-A-Bear Workshop at Potomac Mills – 703-499-8220/www.buildabear.com/C: **Call**

Build-A-Bear Workshop at Tysons Corner Center – 703-448-2327/www.buildabear.com/C: **Call**

Cabell's Mill – Centreville – 703-938-8835/ www.fairfaxcounty.gov/parks/weddings.htm/ C: **cws**

Café Marianna – Alexandria – 703-519-3776/ www.cafemarianna.com/C: 80

Carlyle House – Alexandria – 703-549-2997/C: **Call**

Cherry Blossom Riverboat – Alexandria – 703-684-0580/ www.potomacriverboatco.com/ C: 400

City of Fairfax "Old Town Hall" – 703-385-7893/ C: **Call**

Clarendon Ballroom - Arlington – 703-469-2244/ www.clarendonballroom.com/C: **cws**

Clark House – Falls Church – 703-938-8835/ www.fairfaxcounty.gov/parks/weddings.htm/ C: **cws**

Clay Café Studios – Falls Church/Fairfax – 703-690-7666/www.claywire.com/C: **cws**

Clyde's – Mark Center – Alexandria – 703-820-8300/ www.clydes.com/C: **Call**

Clyde's – Tysons Corner – 703-734-1907/ www.clydes.com/C: **Call**

Collingwood-on-the-Potomac – Alexandria – 703-765-1652/C: 150

Cruise Ship Dandy – Alexandria – 703-683-6076/ www.dandydinnerboat.com/C: **cws**

Dranesville Tavern – Dranesville – 703-938-8835/ www.fairfaxcounty.gov/parks/weddings.htm/ C: **Call**

Evergreen Country Club – Haymarket – 703-754-4125/www.evergreencc.org/C: **cws**

Fairfax Historic Property Rental – Several Locations – 703-938-8835, 703-750-1598

Fire Hall Rentals/Loudoun County Convention & Visitors Bureau – 703-771-7525, ext. 13

Foxchase Manor – Fairfax – 703-369-3638/ www.foxchasemanor.com/C: 300

Gadsby's Tavern – Alexandria – 703-548-1288/ www.gadsbystavernrestaurant.com/C: 300

The Goodstone Inn – Middleburg – 540-687-4645/ www.goodstone.com/C: **cws**

Great Falls Grange – Great Falls – 703-938-8835/ www.fairfaxcounty.gov/parks/weddings.htm/ C: **cws**

The Grey Horse Inn – The Plains – 540-253-7000/ www.greyhorseinn.com/C: **Call**

Gunston Hall Plantation – Mason Neck – 703-550-9220/ www.gunstonhall.org/ C: 225 **ID**/1000 **OD**

Heart in Hand – Clifton – 703-830-4111 /www.heartinhandrestaurant.com/C: 150

The Hermitage Inn Restaurant – Clifton – 703-830-0855/ www.hermitageinnrestaurant.com/C: 250

Hilton Mark Center Alexandria – 703-845-1010/C: **Call**

Hilton Springfield – 703-971-8900/C: **Call**

Holiday Inn – Fair Oaks – 703-352-2525/ www.holiday-inn.com/C: **cws**

Holiday Inn/Historic Carradoc Hall – Leesburg – 1-888-850-8545/www.holiday-inn.com/C: 300

Holiday Inn – Reagan National Airport – Arlington – 703-684-7200/ www.holiday-inn.com/C: 250

Holiday Inn Tysons Corner – McLean – 703-893-2100/www.holiday-inn.com/C: **cws**

Holiday Inn Washington Dulles Airport – Dulles – 703-471-7411/www.holiday-inn.com/C: 300

Hunter House – Vienna – 703-938-8835/ www.fairfaxcounty.gov/parks/weddings.htm/C: **Call**

Hyatt Arlington – 703-875-3387/ www.hyatt.com/C: 300

Hyatt Fair Lakes – Fairfax – 703-818-1234/ www.hyatt.com/C: **cws**

Hyatt Regency Reston – 703-709-1234/ www.hyatt.com/C: 1000

The Inn at Vint Hill – 703-330-1717/ www.theinnatvinthill.com/C: **cws**

J.R.'s Festival Lakes – Leesburg – 703-821-0545/ Apr.-Nov./ www.jrspicnics.com/www.jrscustomcatering.com /C: **OD** 6000

J.R.'s Stockyards Inn – Tysons Corner – 703-893-3390/ www.jrsbeef.com/C: 65

Keswick Hall – Keswick – 1-800-274-5391/ www.keswick.com/C: 400

Knights of Columbus – Arlington – 703-536-9656/C: 300

L'Auberge Chez Francois – Great Falls – 703-759-3800/C: 75

La Bergerie – Alexandria – 703-683-1007/ www.labergerie.com/C: 52

Leesburg Animal Park – 703-433-0002/ www.leesburganimalpark.com/C: **Call**

Lightfoot – Leesburg – 703-771-2233/C: **Call**

Luray Caverns, Luray, Va – 540-743-6551/ www.luraycaverns.com/C: **Call**

Made by You, Arlington – 703-841-3533/C: **Call**

Maggiano's Little Italy – McLean – 703-356-9000/ www.maggianos.com/C: 200

The Manor House at White Hall Farm – Bluemont – 703-948-2999/ www.whitehallestate.com/C: 150

Morrison House – Alexandria – 703-838-8000/ www.morrisonhouse.com/C: **Call**

The Mount Vernon Inn– Mount Vernon – 703-780-0011/www.mountvernon.org/C: **cws**

Newtown Grill (Diner) – Centreville – 703-266-1888/ www.sharkclubonline.com/ C: 800

Oasis Winery – Hume – 1-800-304-7656/ www.oasiswine.com/C: 150 **ID**/2500 **OD**

Oatlands Plantation – Leesburg – 703-777-3174/ www.oatlands.org/C: **Call**

Old School House – Great Falls – 703-938-8835/ www.fairfaxcounty.gov/parks/weddings.htm/C: **Call**

Party Places.Virginia – www.childrenparty.com/ partyplaces/virginialist.html/C: **Call**

Pavilions of Turkey Run – McLean – 703-821-0545/April-Oct./C: 1000 **OD**

Potomac Belle Charter Yacht – Alexandria – 703-868-5566/C: 49

Potomac Riverboat Company – Alexandria – 703-684-0580/C: **Call**

Potowmack Landing – Alexandria – 703-548-0001/ www.potowmacklanding.com/ C: **cws**

Quality Hotel & Suites Court House Plaza – Arlington – 703-524-4000/C: **Call**

Radisson Hotel Old Town Alexandria –
703-683-6000/www.radissonoldtown.com/C:400

The Rail Stop – 540-253-5644/C: **Call**

Raspberry Plain – Leesburg – 703-777-1888/C: **Call**

The Richard Johnston Inn – Fredericksburg –
877-557-0770/www.bbonline.com/C: **cws**

The Ritz Carlton – Pentagon City –
703-415-5000/www.ritzcarlton.com/C: 800

The Ritz Carlton – Tysons Corner –
703-506-4300/ www.ritzcarlton.com/C: 1500

River Farm (American Horticultural Society) –
Alexandria – 703-768-5700/C: **ID/OD Call**

Rockledge Mansion – Occoquan –
703-491-6335/C: **Call**

Rose Hill Manor – Leesburg – 703-369-3638/
www.rosehillmanor.com/C: **Call**

Sea Sea & Co. – Occoquan – 703-690-2004/C: **Call**

Sheraton Crystal City Hotel – Arlington –
703-486-1111/www.sheratonhotels.com/C: **Call**

Sheraton Premiere – Tysons Corner –
703-448-1234/www.sheratonhotels.com/C: **Call**

Sheraton Suites Alexandria –
703-836-4700/www.sheratonhotels.com/C: **Call**

Silver Diner – Several Locations/
www.silverdiner.com

Stone Mansion – Alexandria – 703-938-8835/
www.fairfaxcounty.gov/parks/weddings.htm/
C: **Call**

Tarara Winery & Vineyard – Leesburg –
703-771-7100/C: **Call**

Thomas Birkby House – Leesburg –
703-777-2700/C: 300

Top of the Town – Arlington – 703-387-TOWN/
www.topofthetown.net/C: 180

Torpedo Factory Art Center – Alexandria –
703-838-4199, ext. 2/C: 300

Woodlawn Plantation – Alexandria –
703-780-4000/C: **Call**

District of Columbia

1789 – 202-965-1789/www.clydes.com/C: 200

African American Tea Praises – 202-529-2748/
www.teapraises.com/C: **Call**

Andale – 202-783-3133/www.andaledc.com/C: 75

Anderson House – 202-785-1484/Specific
Guidelines Apply/C: 150

Arts Club of Washington – 202-331-7282/C: 150
ID/250 **OD**

Bistro Bis – 202-661-2701/
www.hotelgeorge.com/C: **Call**

Café Milano – 202-333-6183/
www.cafemilanodc.com/C: 60

Capital Children's Museum – 202-675-4120/
www.ccm.org/C: 600

The Capitol Hilton – 202-393-1000/
www.hilton.com/C: **Call**

Carnegie Institution of Washington –
202-387-6400/C: 500

Christian Heurich Mansion – 202-483-3000/C: 350

City Museum of Washington, D.C. –
202-785-2068/www.citymuseumdc.org/C: 800

Clyde's – 202-333-9180/www.clydes.com/C: **cws**

Corcoran Museum of Art – 202-639-1781/C: 1000

The Churchill Hotel – 202-797-2000/C: 300

DAR Constitution Hall – 202-628-4780/C: **Call**

D.C. Coast – 202-216-5988/
www.savvydiner.com/C: 55

Decatur House Museum – 202-842-0917/
www.decaturhouse.org/C: **Call**

Dinosaur Birthday Party – 202-543-1165/
www.glue.umd.edu/~gdouglas/dfund/C: **Call**

Dumbarton House – 202-337-2288 /C: 200

F. Scotts – 202-965-1789/www.clydes.com/C: 125

The Fairmont Washington, D.C. –
202-429-2400/www.fairmont.com/C: 700

Folger Shakespeare Library – 202-675-0324/
www.folger.edu/C: **Call**

Four Seasons Hotel – 202-342-0444/C: **Call**

Galileo – 202-293-7191/C: **Call**

Galleria at Lafayette Center – 202-835-0093/C: **Call**

Goldoni – 202-293-1511/C: **Call**

The Hay Adams Hotel – 202-638-6600/
www.hayadams.com/C: 150

The Henley Park Hotel – 202-638-5200/
www.henleypark.com/C: **cws**

Hilton Washington & Towers – 202-483-3000/
www.hiltons.com/C: **cws**

Hilton Washington Embassy Row – 202-265-1600/
www.hiltons.com/C: **cws**

Hotel George – 202-347-4200/
www.hotelgeorge.com/C: up to 150

Hotel Monaco – 202-628-7177/
www.monaco-dc.com/C: up to 300

Hotel Washington – 202-638-5900/
www.hotelwashington.com/C: 650

International Spy Museum (Catering by Zola) –
202-393-7798/C: 150

The J.W. Marriott – 202-626-6922/
www.marriotthotels.com /C: 1500

The Jefferson Hotel – 202-347-2200/C: 150

Kennedy-Warren Ballrooms – 202-483-2058/C:
450 Kennedy/350 Warren

Kinkead's – 202-296-7700/www.kinkead.com/C: 55

The Latham Hotel – 202-726-5000/
www.thelatham.com/C: 200

Lebanese Taverna Restaurant – 202-265-8681/
C: 60

Loews L'Enfant Plaza Hotel – 202-484-1000/
www.loewshotels.com/C: **cws**

MCI Center – 202-628-3200, ext. 6005/
www.mcicenter.com/C: **Call**

Made By You, Washington – 202-363-9590/
C: **Call**

The Madison Hotel – 202-862-1600, 800-424-
8577/ www.themadison.com/C: 345

Maggiano's D.C. – 202-966-5500/
www.maggianos.com/C: 400

The Mandarin Hotel – 202-554-8588/
www.mandarinoriental.com/C: 900 **+ OD**

Mansion on O Street – 202-496-2000/C: **Call**

Marriott at Metro Center – 202-737-2200/
www.marriotthotels.com/C: 800

Marriott Wardman Park – 202-328-2000/
www.marriotthotels.com/C: **cws**

Martin's of Georgetown – 202-338-6144/C: **Call**

McLean Gardens Ballroom – 202-966-9781/
C: 350

Mellon Auditorium – 202-312-1300/C: 640

Meridian International Center – 202-667-6800/
www.meridian.org/C: 300

Metro Center Grille – 202-824-6122/C: 350

Mexican Cultural Institute – 202-728-1628/C: **Call**

Morrison-Clark Inn – 202-898-1200/
www.morrisonclark.com/C: 200

National Building Museum – 202-272-2448/
C: 2500

National Museum of Women in the Arts –
202-783-5000/C: **Call**

National Park Service/www.nps.gov

National Press Club – 202-662-7522/
www.press.org/C: 1000

Occidental Grill – 202-783-1475/C: **Call**

The Odyssey – 202-488-6010/
www.odysseycruises.com/C: 600

Old Ebbit Grill – 202-347-4800/
www.clydes.com/C: 300

Omni Shoreham Hotel – 202-756-5164/C: **Call**

The Park Hyatt – 202-789-1234/
www.hyatt.com/C: **cws**

Party Places.Washington –
www.childrenparty.com/partyplaces/
washingtondclist.html/C: **Call**

Poste Brasserie – 202-628-7177/
www.monaco-dc.com/C: 40

The Phillips Collection – 202-387-2151/C: 150

Phillips Flagship – 202-488-8515, 1-800-648-7067/
www.phillipsfoods.com/C: 1200

Phoenix Park Hotel – 202-737-9558/
www.phoenixparkhotel.com/C:700

The Prime Rib – 202-466-8811/
www.theprimerib.com/C: 20

The Renaissance Washington, D.C. –
202-638-2626/www.renaissancehotels.com/
C: **cws**

Republic Gardens – 202-232-2710 (Certain
Days/Time)/C: 500

The Ritz Carlton Georgetown – 202-912-4100/
www.ritzcarlton.com/C: 50

The Ritz Carlton Washington, D.C. –
202-974-4900/www.ritzcarlton.com/C: 1100

Ronald Reagan Bldg. & Intl Trade Ctr. –
202-312-1300/www.itcdc.com/C: 1500

Sequoia Restaurant – 202-944-4200/C: 500

Sewall-Belmont House – 202-546-3989/
www.sewallbelmont.org/C: 350

Spirit of Washington Harbor Cruises –
202-554-8013/www.spiritofwashington.com/
C: **Call**

The St. Regis Washington, D.C. – 202-638-2626/
www.starwood.com/C: 200

Swann House – 202-265-4414/
www.swannhouse.com/ C: 75

Tabard Inn – 202-785-1277/C: 60

Taberna Del Alabardero – 202-429-2200/
www.alabardero.com/C: 160

Ten Penh – 202-393-4500/C: **Call**

Tony & Joe's Seafood Place – 202-944-4545/
www.tonyandjoes.com/C: 200

Union Station – 202-289-8300/
www.unionstationevents.com/C: 3500

Vidalia – 202-659-1990/C: 50

Washington National Cathedral –
202-537-5581/C: **Call**

Washington Plaza Hotel – 202-842-1300,
1-800-424-1140/
www.washingtonplazahotel.com/C: 400

The Watergate Hotel – 202-295-4956/
www.thewatergatehotel.com/C: 1000

The Westin Embassy Row – 202-293-2100/
www.westin.com/C: **cws**

The Westin Grand Hotel – 202-429-0100/
C: 250 **+ OD**

Willard Inter-Continental Washington –
202-628-9100/www.washington.interconti.com/
C: 600

Wyndham Washington DC – 202-457-9167/
www.wyndham.com/C: 500

Yanyu – 202-686-6968/C: 12

Zaytinya – 202-638-0800/C: 50

Zola – 202-654-0999/C: 40

Hotel Chains

www.doubletreehotels.com

www.embassysuites.com

www.hiltons.com /1-800-hiltons

www.holiday-inns.com /1-800-holiday

www.hyatt.com

www.loewshotels.com

www.marriotthotels.com/1-800-831-4004

www.radissonhotels.com

www.ramadahotels.com

www.renaissancehotels.com

www.ritzcarlton.com

www.sheratonhotels.com

www.starwoodhotels.com

www.westinhotels.com

www.wyndhamhotels.com

DESTINATION SPOTS AND ORGANIZERS

Atlantis Dive Center – Key Largo, Florida –
1-800-331-DIVE

Diamond Baseball Tours – 1-800-275-1567/
www.diamondbaseballtours.com

Gaela Weddings (Europe) – 804-346-8714/
www.gaelaweddings.com

The Horned Dorset Primavera – Ricon, Puerto Rico –
1-800-633-1857/www.horneddorset.com

Kelly's on the Bay – Key Largo, Florida –
1-800-226-0415/www.kellysonthebay.com

Las Vegas/Jim Ryan – 202-296-5300/
www.vegasfreedom.com

LeSport – St. Lucia – 1-800-544-2883/
www.theromanticholiday.com

Mountain Climbing Weddings/Destination Bride –
Chatham, New York – 518-392-7766

National Parks/www.nps.gov

Pink Beach Cottages – Bermuda –
1-800-355-6161/www.pinkbeach.com

Rendezvous – St. Lucia – 1-800-544-2883/
www.theromanticholiday.com

The Ritz Carlton St. Thomas – 1-340-775-3333/
www.ritzcarlton.com

The Ritz Carlton San Juan Hotel Spa & Casino –
787-253-1700/www.ritzcarlton.com

Roadtrips (Sports) – 800-465-1765/
www.roadtrips.com

Rock & Roll Hall of Fame – Cleveland –
888-764-ROCK (7625) /www.rockhall.com

St. Peters Great House – St. Thomas –
340-774-1724/www.caribbeancelebrations.com

Ski Weddings/www.kunelius.com/skiwed.html

Skydive Orange, Inc. – Fisherville, Virginia –
540-943-6587/www.skydiveorange.com

Skydive Virginia – Louisa, Virginia –
1-800-414-3483/www.skydive-virginia.com

Sky Diving Center at Ocean City, Md.
/www.skydiveoc.com

Sports Travel – 800-662-4424/
www.baseballroadtrips.com

United States Parachute Assoc. – Alexandria, Va. –
703-836-2843/ww.uspa.org

Cruise Lines

www.carnivalcruiselines.com

www.costacruises.com

www.cunard.com

www.hollandamerica.com

www.ncl.com

www.orientcruises.com

www.princesscruises.com

www.rccl.com

www.seagoddess.com

www.windstarcruises.com

MISCELLANEOUS

Ace Beverage – 202-966-4444

Elman Labels & Paper Products (Gift Packaging) –
301-417-9202

Showcase Productions, Inc. (Bridal Shows) –
703-425-1127/www.bridalshowcase.com ◆

NOTES

NOTES

Notes

NOTES